The first thirty

Butleigh Amateur Rugby Football Club

Written by Ashley Maunder

Illustrated by Jeff Farrow

Running Fox

2006

Published by Running Fox
www.runningfox.co.uk

Published in August 2006

Editor: Janet Powell – email janet@runningfox.co.uk

ISBN: 0-95506261-1-6

Cover design and illustrations: Jeff Farrow

Printed by The Somerton Printery. Somerton
Design and layout by Perception Creative Design. Ilminster

Dedication

This book is dedicated with the greatest possible appreciation to the thousands of players, and their supporters, who have played for and against the Butleigh Amateur Rugby Union Football Club. Thank you everyone for the most magnificent, colourful sporting days imaginable.

Acknowledgements

The following people are thanked for their assistance and for their contributions:

The Editor of the *Mid Somerset Series of Newspapers* for permission to use material previously published in the pages of the *Central Somerset Gazette*.

Garvin Davies for permission to reproduce the photograph of the English Women's Rugby Team 1998.

The Bristol Evening Post for permission to reproduce the photograph of Martin Corry and Phillipa Kennedy 1998.

Ian Wooldridge, David Rosser, Tony Spreadbury and John Mallet for the remarks that they have kindly contributed to the foreword of the book.

All those who have donated or loaned photographs of people and events.

I am grateful to Janet Powell for the expert support that she has generously given in project managing the creation of the book. This has enabled me to realise a long held ambition to produce a book concerning the exploits of the Butleigh Amateurs; without her unstinting help it might never have materialised. I extend special thanks to the quite brilliant Jeff Farrow for his inspired work in producing so many terrific illustrations. I also wish to acknowledge the contributions of Chris Harding, Tony Berkeley, Simon Donnelley, Dr Tim Walker, Andy Nixon, Peter Farrant and Dennis Powell. Thanks also to the wonderful support, over seven patient years, of the Sports Editors who waited, often hours over deadline, for the hand scribbled reports to arrive on their desks. My grateful thanks go to Adam Maunder for his imaginative contributions towards the concept of some of the illustrations and to Alison Richards for so thoughtfully keeping a record of Butleigh's days out – especially when the Author often returned home later than anticipated.

I have depended upon anecdotes and recollections from many sources. Any errors of fact or interpretation are entirely my own.

Ashley Maunder - *Kingweston 2006*

Editor's note

In November 2005 Ashley told me that for some time he had been thinking about producing a book to celebrate the 30th year of Butleigh Amateur Rugby Union Football Club. I believed that making such a book would simply mean collecting the best of Ashley's newspaper reports and linking them together with text and illustrations. As it turned out, this was not quite the case. Putting the book together became an organic process – rather like the development of the club itself. Organic growth is natural and wholesome and no artificial additives or preservatives are used in the process but the result may not necessarily conform to expectations. This book is as fresh and tasty as the produce from a good farm shop. No pigs were hurt in the incidents described

Janet Powell - *Barton St David 2006*

Foreword

Let me warmly endorse the command of Mike Stone that appears early on in this publication. Apparently after some arduous activity on the rugby pitch, followed by vigorously tending the bar, he suffered a heart attack. As he was being stretchered out, he waved and yelled: 'Sorry, lads, carry on. Don't for goodness sake stop now.' Truly Churchillian.

To my shame I had never heard of Butleigh Amateur Rugby Football Club until I was contacted by Chris Harding, an old friend. Its story enthrals me. Amateur is the key word. Penniless, still living off its wits, defying political correctness to the point of cheerful anarchy, it is now raising money not only for itself but for needy charities.

I have spent 45 years of my life reporting sport, including rugby union. Its adoption of professionalism was inevitable but its paranoiac obsession with stacking up more and more money has utterly divorced it from the genuine grass roots of a lovely, tough, character-building game.

Butleigh's emergence nostalgically reminds me of the days when you paid a two-bob match fee and split the beer money afterwards. I thought they had gone. They haven't, thank goodness. As Mike Stone said: 'Don't stop now.'

Ian Wooldridge - *The Daily Mail*

It has always been my ambition to referee at every club in Somerset before I retire. I shall never forget my appearance at Butleigh for it was there that I sent off twelve players in a most uncontroversial manner. It was a Sunday morning game and the players were exhibiting more enthusiasm than skill. It is the role of the referee to give the thirty players the best game possible. This particular match demanded more creative decisions than I can remember making in any high level game. It was hard work but great fun.

In the closing seconds of the game there was a scrum in the centre of the field. I instructed the scrum halves to delay the put in and to ensure the whole scrum was straight. With that, I signalled desperately to the three quarters to leave the field immediately. The forwards were left totally unaware of their departure. The ball was put in with the scrum halves earnestly encouraging their weighty companions to secure the ball with more pushing. Eventually the ball came out, the scrum broke up for them all to find an otherwise empty pitch. That was full time. I'd always wanted to do that.

What a wonderful club to visit. Enjoy the book!

Tony Spreadbury - *International Referee*

Despite what you read about premierships and professionalism, the Butleigh Amateur Rugby Football Club stands squarely in the mainstream tradition of English rugby, a tradition that many years ago Michael Green celebrated through the magnificent Bagford Vipers Extra B in his 'Art of Coarse Rugby' ('a game played by fewer than 15 a side, at least half of whom should be totally unfit'). It's a tradition that lives joyfully on, though sadly not at the top level of the game.

Crucially the pub is as much a part of the game as the playing pitch; that beer and real rugby are more or less synonymous goes some way to explain the atmosphere of creative anarchy that surrounds the enterprise. Practical arrangements seem to owe a good deal to the principles of Heath-Robinson, the games themselves are a triumph of hope over experience, but the essence is in the camaraderie which, in Butleigh's case especially, allows full rein to an entertaining range of colourfully unpredictable characters.

Pierre Rives thought that 'the whole point of rugby is that it is, first and foremost, a state of mind, a spirit.' Well, he is French, and he may have been referring to a state of mind that Butleigh Amateurs would recognise, but in a more Anglo-Saxon idiom Dick Greenwood got it right when he said that, in his considered opinion, 'the amateur rugby union player has an inalienable right to play like a pillock'. And why not?

Fans of Ashley Maunder's reports in the *Central Somerset Gazette* will be grateful for this further contribution to the literature, anthropology and social history of Somerset, and will know what to expect; new readers are in for a treat.

David Rosser - *England and Wasps Player*

In May 2003 I played my last game in a European Shield final in front of 30,000 supporters. The day went something like this:

7.00am – breakfast at a luxury hotel. 8.00am – autograph session, 9.00am – physio session and massage, 10.00am – warm up with fitness experts, 11.00am lineout meeting, 11.30am – team meeting, 12.30pm – team warm up, 2.30pm – lose the game (28 – 12), 5.00pm – go home miserable!

My next game was for Butleigh Amateurs:

2.45pm – arrive for a 2.30 kick off. Drink mulled wine. 3.00pm – play, laugh, enjoy, 4.30pm – sheep dip bath, cider. Go home very happy – can't remember the score!

Vive la difference!!! Enjoy this book.

John Mallet - *England and Bath Player and sometime Butleigh Amateur*

Contents

1. The Early Days

They only want the posts...

During the drought stricken months of 1976, a particularly thirsty time, a seam of school leavers rallied most evenings in the magnificent Rose and Portcullis Public House in the Somerset village of Butleigh. From this gathering, games of football, cricket and eventually rugby were organized. After playing two games of rugby amongst ourselves on the Millfield 1st XV pitches at Kingweston playing field (the very one Gareth Edwards, J.P.R. Williams and Richard Harding ran out on as pupils), opposition was sought.

Butleigh full-back Thomas Gillam, whose athletic prowess included horizontal trampolining with a young lady at nearby Lytes Cary Manor, thought that Sherborne socialite Tom Kelly might rally a team. Four games and four wins later against the Plume of Feathers and the die was cast - Butleigh Rugby Football Club was formed. Tom Kelly, who captained the Feathers quite majestically for two seasons, then fell from office by downgrading his side into becoming Sherborne Rugby Club.

The following season new teams adorned Butleigh's fixture list, the most intriguing being Tone Vale Psychiatric Hospital away. This fixture was a revelation since Sunday opening hours, at this time, were from twelve to two and then seven to ten thirty. At Tone Vale the staff bar was open all day. Mike Stone who organized the matches was also the bar steward and he excelled with the after-match hospitality. Following a match in which he had played he was some way through the after match celebrations when struck down by a heart attack. Cheerful as ever, waving farewell as he was being stretchered out, he said,

'Sorry about this lads, carry on. Don't for goodness sake stop now'.

Tone Vale away was a wonderful fixture apart from keeping an eye out for the occasional patient wandering onto the pitch. Butleigh always won except for one occasion when, on turning up for the usual comfortable run-out, we found that Tone Vale had invited the somewhat unyielding, a lot less friendly, bone-grinding Wiveliscombe Rugby Club to represent them. Butleigh didn't win that day.

When games began to be played every month Butleigh had to find their own pitch as Millfield took down their posts at the end of the rugby term in December. A fifty-acre dairy field running alongside the Millfield playing field seemed ideal. To begin with, lines were scraped out using a large U-shaped branch fallen from a nearby beech tree. However technological advances were quickly made. Using the farmer's tractor an iron bar was forced down through the pick up hitch and the tractor driven at pace up and down the field gouging out the touch lines. For rugby posts, Millfield kept a supply of wooden uprights and crossbars tucked along the inside of the nearby fence separating their playing fields from the pasture land and, having climbed gingerly over the barbed wire fence, we borrowed two sets of posts and crossbars necessary for each game. Digging holes to place the posts was a daunting task. After eighteen inches, soil gave way to limestone rock and despite hammerings with a crow-bar it was impossible to plant the posts deeply enough.

With the posts and crossbars lashed together with yellow bailer-twine, the day's teams would push the framework into the holes and up into the air. Particularly unpredictable on gusting, windy days, spectators would be encouraged to stand next to the upright taking a firm hold when play approached. In recognition of the potential for disaster, scrums would be moved away from the toppling zone. Occasionally the posts would blow over during a game and have to be reset. Butleigh lock forward Tony Phelps felt that this aided attempts at making conversions.

Sharing the pitch with Butleigh Rugby Club was a herd of dairy cows with a bull 'Frankenstein'. One of the grounds-man's early tasks was to shoo the cows off the pitch and then shovel up the pats. The problem was that cows are naturally inquisitive by nature. As soon as someone appeared to prepare the pitch so the herd would come over to investigate, tails swishing and lifting at will. If the bull found courtship irresistible during this phase of operations, the match would be delayed until the affair was resolved and he could be encouraged to another part of the field.

In the late seventies and early eighties several events occurred that were to be significant in the development of the club. In 1981, still with no clubhouse to change in, the Butleigh club was offered the opportunity of moving to Kingweston Village Green sports field complete with its own cricket pavilion built in 1919 and somewhat neglected over the decades - absolute luxury!

Crucial to Butleigh's social and playing scene at this time was the arrival of Captain Tony Berkeley. An ex-Blackheath 1st team fly-half and a merchant-seaman, he played the guitar and was in command of an endless list of wet-weather songs. Butleigh days out were never the same thereafter. In place of more ordinary entertainment, Berkeley held court and a repertoire of colourful songs has followed ever since.

In 1979 Butleigh number eight Robin Reid moved to Southern Spain for a year as part of his Spanish degree course. He sent back news of an expanding rugby scene over there. Within months Reid brought over a team from Seville and four weeks later Butleigh made the return trip. The brilliant weather and generous hospitality grew and, until recently, the clubs exchanged fixtures every two or three years. Butleigh RFC now ventures even further afield into the Southern Hemisphere.

Early Butleigh strip.

By 1980 the fixture list had increased to fourteen games a season and to our astonishment we found ourselves not only in the Somerset Handbook but also in the Somerset Knockout Cup competition drawn that year against Taunton away. After a terrific battle Taunton won 24-12. The organizers of the Cup competition possibly believed (many still do) that the Butleigh club was bereft of any home facilities because for the next few years we were continually drawn away, always against a top Somerset club and always a cracking day out. Forms from the Somerset RFU also started appearing through the door at the Rose and Portcullis. After refreshments these were joyously filled in so that, without any verification, the handbook stated that Butleigh fielded five senior teams, under 21s, under 19s, colts and minis as well as possessing several pitches, two with floodlights, one grandstand and several scrummaging machines. All this information was duly processed and printed in the RFU Handbook making Butleigh appear as big a side as Bath or Bristol. The plus side was that, in all innocence, Butleigh started to receive a generous allocation of tickets for Internationals; the downside was a stream of calls from clubs wishing to play our colts and minis. Fortunately in 1981, as Chris Harding mentions later, the Secretary stepped in, 'putting an end to all this nonsense', and he set about creating a less strained relationship with the RFU.

Another key element in Butleigh's history was meeting up with local Rugby team, Tor RFC, in Glastonbury. In 1978 the Butleigh team was invited to play a pre-season warm up game against Tor. Butleigh lost 34-12. Nothing could compare to the hospitality shown after the match with large schooners of sherry at give-away prices and beer half the price of anywhere else. A spectacular friendship was created between the two clubs. Such was the distraction of the occasion that a Butleigh wing forward attempted to bypass the Street roundabout and drove through a set of wooden railings on a shortcut home. The police and a doctor were quickly on the scene. The slightly dazed player was able to whisper to the doctor that his uncertain state and that of the others on board was due more to Tor's hospitality than to any injury sustained from the unexpected incident of leaving the road. The doctor drove the player and passengers home and the police moved on.

Butleigh RFC exists on a zero bank balance. The club has no money and owes no money. Any crises of cash are met by occasional match fees and whip-rounds. This possibly makes the club one of the wealthier ones in the country. Committee meetings may be called at a moment's notice when two or more are gathered together drinking beer; nothing written down and nothing, for fear of affecting the enjoyment of the beer, controversial to be discussed. As a result of this freedom, unexpected developments can occur without the rest of the club members knowing.

In 1995, Honorary Secretary Chris Harding took himself off to the NEC in Birmingham and spoke heroically in front of seven hundred delegates against professionalism in rugby and the destabilizing effect of leagues on a much loved amateur sport. Many of the problems he foresaw, including players leaving the game and successful clubs overstretching their financial abilities because of the costs involved in more extensive travelling, have been sadly realized.

However, the ethos of playing good team rugby has never dimmed nor diminished. Every match represents a day packed with the uncertainty of who is going to play, how good are the opposition and how will these precious hours unfold? It is very much a theatre of our own making, one which to date has stood the test of time.

The Season begins.

2. Clubhouse and Ground

J.R. FARROW 2005

Having played for three years on a meadow, with maintenance no more than scraping pats off the playing surface and marking the pitch out with a crowbar stuffed between a tractor pickup hitch, a village green in nearby Kingweston, formerly used by the Cricket Club became available. Not only a pitch but a small, wooden, cricket pavilion complete with electricity and mains water supply and the accompanying luxury of a visitors' changing hut.

It took SWEB ten months to cut off the electricity; however Wessex Water allowed Butleigh nearly three years of unpaid bills before taking similar action. After-match washing facilities were afforded by the changing block of nearby Millfield School boarding house, Kingweston House, until a change of House Master, from rugger supporter Eric Westwell to hockey enthusiast Tim Wilbur, meant that a change had to be made. Fortunately there was a back up facility - a galvanized cattle trough some one hundred yards from the clubhouse in a nearby field which, though bracing to wash in, was effective. There was also a tap on the trough that could trail water through a garden hosepipe the one hundred yards to the clubhouse where the remaining length, loosely coiled, would warm up nicely during the early and later months of the season. To accommodate this feature, home games were encouraged towards September/October and April/May with away matches arranged particularly during the frozen months of January and February. Unfortunately the pipe, due to being run over by cars on match days, sprang severe leaks and this system became increasingly more disappointing towards the end of the season. The principle of showering improved in the 1990s when the club used nearby village Barton St. David's changing rooms. However, due to rugby always kicking off late, whenever rugby days clashed with football the hot water had been used by the time of our arrival.

The Bath with Tim Gelfs, James Timms and James Phillips.

The Dynanometer and beyond

The arrival in Butleigh in the mid 1990's of former Swanage and Wareham 1st team prop-forward, and South Barrow Dairy Farmer, Andy Nixon, changed matters beyond recognition. For Sunday morning home matches Nixon would borrow a Dynanometer from local agricultural merchants, Tinknells of Galhampton, and drive it on the back of his tractor pick-up hitch five miles to Butleigh's ground.

A Dynanometer is a large, friction-creating device that runs off the power take-off shaft on the back of tractors and it is used to test the horsepower output of tractor engines to see how efficiently they are running. Linking up to mains water, the water running through the Dynanometer acts as friction resistance to the tractor engine. The by-product of this intricate test is white hot water which fountains out of an outlet pipe. In Butleigh's case it was directed into a four hundred gallon trough newly located on the side of the clubhouse changing rooms. Taking about forty-five minutes to fill the bath this system worked quite brilliantly and teams that had declined to visit Butleigh due to thier perceived lack of facilities started to reappear. The bath itself is civilized beyond belief and can hold up to thirteen people where drinks are often served after matches. The view across mid Somerset farmland from the wide open corrugated door is sublime; or it was, until the day of the incident.

Nixon would drive the Dynanometer over to the pitch on his medium-sized runabout Ferguson tractor before linking it up to Kingweston farmer Harvey Maunder's top of the range, size of a small hotel, Massey Ferguson 625 tractor. Unknown to the operator, one fateful Sunday, the large tractor had enjoyed a midweek service and consequently was powering out an unusually high level of horsepower. With mains water being fed into the Dynanometer the revs of the tractor were increased to maximum and an increased level of horsepower was being generated. 'Ey up!' said Nixon looking at the white clouds of steam bellowing out of the bath, 'It's going well today'.

Within minutes, accompanied by grunting reverberations and unusual hammering vibrations, a floor show of explosive rivets and washers began flying off the Dynanometer accompanied by blue oil spurts and black smoke. The machine was patched up and returned as usual to Tinknells the following day. Some weeks later a phone call to see if the machine could once more be borrowed led to the harrowing tale that someone else had hired it and the Dynanometer had blown up ten minutes into the test. Some time later, having initially been offered to Butleigh in its prime for £1,500, it sold at auction fetching £60.

Such had been the delight of the 400 gallon cattle trough filled with hot Radox-bubbled water that something new had to be improvised quickly. Although Wessex Water had linked the club to the mains, after payment of a £380 bill, the new meter was happily buried under a foot of clay soil. Over a beer, local farmer Dave Fry who has access to an amazing range of goods, mentioned that he had a disused chicken dip tank, slightly worn, we could have for nothing.

The dip tank is a high-sided, narrow, rectangular container and the water is heated by propane gas. The practicalities are that having unscrewed the propane release valve, raw gas hisses into a metal tube running through the base of the 150 gallon tank. Before too much gas fills the pipe it is vital to ignite the highly volatile situation. Too much gas and there is a forceful explosion that snaffles out the flame, singeing the hairs off the lighting arm and requiring a second match. When alight in full roaring throttle the sound is reminiscent of a hot air balloon attempting lift off or a harrier jet at nearby Yeovilton Airbase preparing for vertical take off. The original purpose of the tank was to pluck table chickens by dipping them in hot water to loosen the feathers from the skin before being plucked. The tank must have had millions of chickens go through it before being retired. The tank was donated to the club because the main heating pipe had a significant hole in its length. This was repaired by Butleigh lock forward and local engineer Harry Buckle Snr. Following vital welding the tank was fork-lifted onto a six pallet high stand resting against the corrugated sheeting portion that separates the bath from the changing room. The hot-water system needs igniting three hours before kick-off to supply three tanks of hot water to fill the bath. It takes a bit of orchestrating since an overhanging oak tree tends to block up the outlet pipe with acorns and twig debris but overall it works better than it should. Ideally a second dip tank sited behind the clubhouse would not only halve the time to heat the water but the volume of noise emanating from two burners might possibly unnerve visiting teams.

The visitors changing room is a different matter - there isn't one anymore - it's gone. There used to be one - quite a classy affair compared to the home team's open-all-hours club house. It used to have panes of glass in the windows, the roof didn't leak and often as not there was a fresh bale of straw to sit on; until one fateful night, when the Butleigh President, one of the more responsible members of the club, a figure head who had tendencies towards pyromania, realised that the bonfire to one side of the pitch was fading. Being a man of decision he walked purposefully over to the visitor's changing facility and pulled off the front entrance door to feed the flames, followed by the wooden framed outer walls and, an hour later, the now collapsed roof. Ever since, visitors have been offered a half of the home team's clubhouse (the side that leaks most) which in many respects is a far more sociable arrangement.

Hunters hunted

Butleigh's pitch is a wide undulating affair pock marked with rabbit holes. The undulations are due to the under-lying drain passages of 18th century stone culverts which have gradually subsided over the years. There is a thought that a well-fed pack of forwards could disappear dramatically one day. The rabbit holes are usually filled in before matches with bags of Somerset peat. In the eighties there wasn't a rabbit problem as many of the team possessed shot guns carried  rather casually behind the seats of cars and vans. With the change in gun regulations the old approach of leaving the Rose and Portcullis public house at closing time and heading off to the rugby ground at midnight to race around the pitch letting off volleys of gun shot the nights before a big game came to a dramatic end. One evening an incident-packed shoot out took place and Kingweston Assistant Housemaster, Chris Harding, became involved.

A group left the Rose and Portcullis to go on a late night pitch hunt with winger Matthew Laver in the back of Home Farm's Polski Fiat pick-up truck and wing forward Paul Panton in the passenger seat. With guns loaded the van raced up from Butleigh along the Kingweston House drive and, in preparation for the sweep of the pitch, took to the school lawns weaving in and out of the laurel bushes in search of game when something was spotted in the headlights scurrying away. Two barrels later not only had something been blown twenty yards into the distance but a number of lights had come on in the main House. As Laver dashed out to collect the fallen game (a hedgehog) a figure appeared through the house archway running straight for the van. Suggestions of firing shots across the Assistant House Master's bow were reluctantly dismissed as the hunters raced off across the lawns, narrowly evading Harding's clutches and down into the village executing a one hundred and eighty degree turn coming back up the road again. Car lights appeared from a quarter of a mile ahead as the vehicles converged. The pursuing House Master chose, correctly, to swerve off the road in his 2CV. The villains of the night raced back to the pub in Butleigh where vehicles were changed and guns broken and hidden. They drove off in a new vehicle to lie low for the night. Hauled the next day before the school authorities (no police action taken) to explain themselves, the shotgun method of pest control was suspended.

More recently three ferrets have been acquired and rabbits that have been caught grazing and digging on the pitch may now be purchased from the local farm shop.

Head grounds man – Stephen Gillam

Gillam is six feet tall, has black, curly hair and moustache, he's genetically thin but is actually quite large, grizzled, and encyclopaedic of mind and has an amazing memory for the trivial details of life. He's a passionate Blues player with a string of feisty girl friends. Butleigh's 1st choice full back (following early retirement of his older brother) until 1986, prodigious

Assistant groundsman - Timmy.

athletic distance runner, prepared for French O level oral exam with five pints of Courage bitter at the Street Inn prior to that afternoon's exam, went in and came out with confidence. 'I thought it went well. I knew what I was talking about. I thought the examiner caught a fair grasp of it as well.'

Vocalist and harmonica player in an up tempo Blues band 'Hogwash Junction Function', he prepared for International matches as a player with a balanced number of brandy sharpeners in the build up to the game. He's currently employed to great effect as green keeper at Wells Golf course and head grounds-man for Butleigh Rugby Club.

Gillam's approach is to prepare in August, in the build up to the Magnificent 7's rugby tournament, an impeccable pitch more perfectly presented than Twickenham – straight white lines within carefully mown strips, flag posts fluttering at every pitch junction. Rolled, wide lane swathes of trimmed grass as broad as carriage ways lay as dark and light shades of green – immaculate pitch presentation. Then that's it for the year. The grass grows – by the end of the season it's knee length deep which does nevertheless offer an effective tactic of steadying up some of the quicker sides.

Gillam became, paradoxically, the toast of the grounds-man of the year awards dinner following his end of season success in bringing a formerly fleet of foot, International Spanish touring side to its knees following months of careful neglect to the pitch. Then of course there is the dilemma of the Somerset Cup competitions when home team pitches have to pass a pre-match referees inspection. In November, 1999, because of an unexpectedly successful cup run within an amazing series of home draws (partly responsible for the club captain's conversion to religion), the grass was already shin high. A call to the head grounds-man was initially given short shrift. 'Look, I've got a lot on at the moment, bring on the sheep.'

18

Local farmer Harvey Maunder came to the rescue when he re-routed his 54 strong beef suckler herd on to the ground.

'I was going to strip graze it starting from the in goal area,' he happily declared, 'but there was so much grazing there I just let them straight at it.' With four days to the 2nd round with the Imperial RFC and whilst applauding the farmer's initiative on the husbandry side there were landmarks of the agreeable occupation everywhere. Also quite unexpectedly there was evidence of the happy news of two calvings, just beyond the village side of the halfway line, giving the appearance that the last home match had developed into bloody, brutal conflict. The disappearance of the goal post protectors, eight bales of hay strapped to the uprights was also a cause for concern. President Tony Berkeley was adamant. 'We can't play on that pitch, the referee will never allow it – we'll play it at Tor Rugby club instead.'

This galvanised the ground staff into prodigious action. Legendary plant hire contractor Dick Fear, said 'No problem, I've got just the beast, a splurge engulfer – a super powerful sewage sucker,' - which it did, leaving a pitch marked with several hundred grassless but pat less cavities.

Hospitality

As regards after match hospitality, the excellent Rose and Portcullis public house in Butleigh has, over three decades and four changes of landlord, been patient, generous and forgiving. The first landlord, Ian Mason (who originally met the future Butleigh captain in Glastonbury Magistrates Court, when one was applying for and receiving his pub license and the other forfeiting his driving license) was a former captain of Bournemouth Rugby Club. In 1976 this coincided with Butleigh starting as a club. Three years later Geoff Hicks, a young landlord from Weston-Super-Mare, came to the Rose and Portcullis

The Rose and Portcullis.

Singing at the Rose and Portcullis.

and, although only playing in a handful of matches, he revelled in the rugby social scene. In the last fourteen years the clubhouse was in the calmer, more dignified custody of Paul Tuckett and David Gardner. David and Paul retired and, sadly, David died earlier this year. Tony Perrone is the current landlord.

Entertainment

With Hicks, on truly excellent days and at a time when the front bar enjoyed a traditional flag stone floor, a combination of after match entertainment would noticeably change the complexion of the pub. A number of dining room tables, for instance, would be gathered in the front bar and with the addition of chairs placed on the tables a Wellington aircraft bomber scene would be enacted with a pilot in charge - usually prop forward Tim Catley-Day - tail and mid section gunners and four players, one from the visiting team placed as engines, encouraged to swing their right arms as propellers flying low over enemy territory. Guns and engines were gradually vocally wiped out by enemy anti aircraft fire. As each engine one by one failed so the pilot would encourage the remaining engines to

Put the fire out!

work harder, turn faster. Eventually only one engine remained, the visitors' representative. The pilot would exhort great revs and greater effort until dramatically the pilot shouted 'Fire, Fire, the engines on fire, put the fire out' and fourteen pints of beer would be thrown over the head of engine number one. On days such as these, especially following Old MacDonald's Farm when the whales were spouting it here there and everywhere, beer would run along the ceiling dribbling a squelch across the floor, out of the front bar into a small hallway and out of the front door and down the main road.

One evening the barman, Murray Eaglesome, was surprised to be kidnapped from behind the bar. Restrained from returning to his duties, he kept calm, saying no more than, 'Come on lads. This isn't very fair. Let me down.' Of course he was released eventually, after the lads had spent some time looking after the bar.

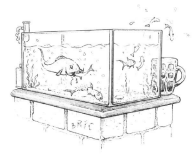

Geoff Hicks, over twelve magnificent years, was marvellous for the club. Although he would occasionally become enraged, he always came round. Introducing a piranha into the pub's tropical fish tank was, despite the disappearance of the Neon fish and the Angel fish's tail becoming increasingly ragged, soon forgiven.

Bonfire Night

This episode took longer to live down. It was Butleigh full back Thomas Gillam's fault. Off to a November fifth Bonfire party he called in for a couple of drinks clutching a box of suspiciously unmarked fireworks. Three drinks later and inquisitiveness had led to a small firework being extracted and placed in a beer bottle on the nearby hearth and the fuse set aglow - a sparkling affair - bright - some smoke, nothing elaborate. A bigger firework was then chosen and placed in an empty wine bottle - this time in the middle of the room. In the ensuing confusion there was a certain disorientation as the landlord, upstairs watching television, hearing screams rushed down to the lounge now filled with acrid white smoke convinced the distant kitchen had gone up. A couple of strangers who had arrived for a quiet drink sat transfixed with terror in the front bar as a choking, gushing cocktail of volcanic properties whooshed out of the impressive firework accompanied by intermittent explosions of red, gold and silver meteorites fizzing and ricocheting off the ceiling and walls, some hurtling into the no-smoking dining area. The main problem lay in the sensitive nature of the new, garish, red, front-bar carpet. Around the base of the wine bottle which by now held just the smouldering remnants of the vigorous display, and despite the manufacturer's claim that the carpet was fireproof, was a perfect carbonized blackened ring of charcoalized carpet pile.

The feast and pantomime

This annual event takes place at Christmas and it is staged in the skittle alley of the Rose and Portcullis. On 6th January 2000, Ashley's report in the *Central Somerset Gazette* describes one of these functions and follows this with an account of the match between Butleigh Amateurs and North Wootton.

The Feast

Before

After

Secretary's Spoof

Chris Harding was given to devising spoofs and many of these were planned beside the bar in The Rose and Portcullis. One of the best was the April Fool joke that he played on leading national newspapers in the mid 1990s. A fax was sent to all of them on 30th March giving details about a new type of rugby being pioneered by the Butleigh club. It was a game of 20 a side, returning to the roots of the game. Play would be for 20 minute quarters; there was to be a traditional scrum with two sets of running backs and adjustments to the offside rule thus giving a faster game. David Hands of *The Times*, on the 1st April, quietly included the gist of this in his match report on Orrel vs Leicester.

The same day, the new editor of *The Times* stated that under his editorship the April Fool hoaxes, for which the paper had been famous, would be no more. He thought they were silly. Harding responded with a letter to explain that his spoof had been successfully published. Mystified, the letters page editor phoned to ask Harding where in the paper the spoof could be found. When the letters page editor discovered that the spoof had been sent by fax, he said, 'That is extremely irresponsible of you.'

'And it is extremely irresponsible of your editor to throw down the gauntlet to the likes of me,' was Harding's retort. The phone was slammed down. Chuckling, Harding thought that was it but there was more to come. Two days later, calls were received from *The Telegraph* and *The Independent* enquiring for details of the new game. Harding joyously shouted down the phone, 'APRIL FOOL'.

A week later, he received a letter from the Sports Editor of *The Times* saying, 'Congratulations on the April Fool. Our editor doesn't understand such things.' So the story must have circulated around the newspaper world of Fleet Street.

Butleigh show how to throw a good spread

| Butleigh Amateurs | 17 |
| North Wootton | 34 |

A reworking of the children's fairy-tale The Three Billy Goats Gruff by Snodgrass White on December 30, at the Rose and Portcullis, was successful enough to encourage further broadening of pantomime themes.

Three vibrant young ladies played the goats while Hamblin, Harse and Wright (played by Chris English) enacted three salacious trolls in a portrayal of subtle vocal interplay and romance set in a nightclub. In the script Harse (a victim of Saturday night misunderstandings in the real world) was

banned from the club for foul play. Wright was forced to leave on medical grounds but Hamblin won over his goat, Miss Wendy Trott, in a clever re-enactment of an actual event that had occurred some years before.

An hour beforehand, the feast had set new standards of good behaviour. The 100 guests had sat noisily but restrained for 20 tension-ripping minutes before the first sprout was idly tossed down the length of the 40ft dining table. Within seconds horizons dimmed as clouds of leftover parsnips, carrots and gravy-lined plates streamed up and down the dining table, ricochet-

ing and splattering off the low ceiling.

The more experienced diners, dressed in black bin liners, whipped out umbrellas. At one end of the alley the audio effect of cold roast potatoes thudding into woodwork was reminiscent of Stephen Spielberg's harrowing epic Saving Private Ryan. This included an unfortunate incident of vivid realism as feast veteran and local solicitor, Colin Dickens, who has played just once on the wing in a 24-year association with Butleigh, against the Plume of Feathers on a rain-lashed Sunday in 1979, was struck on the very bridge of his glasses by a stray,

Clipping from the Mid Somerset Newspapers January 6, 2000.

meteoric, well braised roaster, leaving him without spectacles, with blurred vision and a gentle ebb of blood seeping down one side of his nose.

The rugby match, played in a steady drizzle, refereed by Tor rugby chairman Tim Kelly, proved too much for some Butleigh players. Hooker John Hunt frustratingly locked his keys and kit in his car minutes before kick-off and impact tackler Andy Nixon failed to secure a vehicle to drive over from his farm near Sherborne.

"The only time the car is there," he later explained through gritted teeth, "is when it needs petrol or

servicing."

The parking area in front of the pitch now gives the impossible hint that Butleigh are utilising it as a gruelling training ground, but in reality the muddied carnage is due to numerous vehicles optimistically slewing the vital energy-saving 30 metres from the sound of a tarmac road to spin as close as possible to the clubhouse door.

While applauding this initiative, it is making heavier work of negotiating the pitch from the changing room.

The game, a titanic affair, was won by the younger, better looking team.

An evening at the Rose and Portcullis.

The Landlords 2005

Butleigh Sevens Team, 2005

Somerset Cup Match vs Blagdon, 2004. Won 25-10

Tour of South Africa, 2006

Butleigh Rugby Giants

Leigh Baker vs Puerto, 1990   *(photo Alan Fincher)*

Margo, 2006

3. Officers and Players

Club Secretary – Chris Harding

One winter's night in 1983, the club captain found himself in the company of Chris Harding, Butleigh's home match referee, at the Rose and Portcullis headquarters. Chris was an experienced rugger bugger in the true tradition of the game. He had been well-schooled in his youth and knew enough rugby songs to keep a party running for hours. He laid claim to having played with Michael Green, the author of 'The Art of Coarse Rugby'. He played and refereed to a modest level, indeed, he had refereed a County game, Dorset Farmers vs. Wiltshire Farmers, and he had been seen on Rugby Special running the line at Twickenham. Who could be better qualified to be official administrator of the club?

Lance Bombardier Chris Harding had done his National Service in the Royal Artillery. He was excused boots due to bunions but played as centre for his regiment. In civilian life he worked as a representative before following an attractive young lady to Africa – Southern Rhodesia now Zimbabwe. Chris loved the place so much that he stayed for seven years before fleeing from another pretty young lady back to England where he took up a variety of occupations including driving coaches to the continent, lambing sheep in the middle of Wiltshire and doing casual work anywhere.

At the age of thirty two he took a short holiday and walked from Bath to Reading along the old canal waterways during which he made a decision to go to St Luke's College, University of Exeter - the famous rugby centre of excellence. During his time there Chris took athletics seriously, competed in the decathlon and refereed rugby. After graduating from St Luke's with a third class honours degree, Harding was appointed to teach geography at Millfield School. Headmaster, Colin Atkinson, gave Harding the seal of approval because he appreciated staff who had benefited from life's experiences. The Head may also have noted Chris's coach driving achievements. Atkinson's own father had been a tram driver in Newcastle.

Harding taught his subject, organised the cross country team and was in charge of junior discipline as well as being Assistant House Master at the Kingweston boarding house. 'Master in charge of junior discipline'- it was just what Butleigh needed, a little formality regarding the responsible side of being a rugby club. It only remained for Ashley to persuade Chris that he was the ideal candidate and, on that winter's night, he succeeded in doing so. Harding recalls,

'After purchasing an inappropriately expensive round of drinks, Ashley struck. He told me tales of woe related to the ill-fortunes of the club. He bemoaned the lack of co-operation among members; he expressed his fears for the future; he told how the fixtures list needed continuity and vision. The sympathetic ear listened in awe and when the question, 'Would you like to be our fixtures secretary?' was put, the set-up was complete and the target responded, with alacrity, in the affirmative. So a happy evening was concluded and nearly a quarter of a century of discreet administration began.'

It was not long before Harding realised the extent of the job he had undertaken. The organisation of fixtures was but a minor part and he soon took up full secretarial duties by default. It was Harding who formalised Butleigh's first committee meetings. 'It's very straight forward,' he explained, 'anyone can hold a meeting at any time, anywhere. The rule is two or more gathered together drinking beer, nothing written down.'

This splendid arrangement had to be fine-tuned several years later when Butleigh hooker Mark Wilkinson called an impromptu meeting and suggested the secretary should be sacked for changing the club name to 'Butleigh Amateur RFC'. Subsequently, the rules for a committee meeting were adjusted to – 'two or more gathered together, drinking beer, nothing written down, and nothing controversial to be discussed'.

Harding, being based at Kingweston where Butleigh home ground is situated, was able to allow vital access to after-match showers in the boarding house. He would also referee for nothing. As referee, Harding's expenses at the end of the game consisted of the referee's pint. Of course he brought a whistle and, if Butleigh were short, he could provide the occasional extremely useful Millfield rugby player from the house. His refereeing could occasionally be alarming. On one occasion, vehemently blasting his whistle, he grabbed the miscreant and exclaimed,

'That's it; I've had enough, out - come on, out of there.'

Pulling the nonplussed player out of the scrum and handing him the whistle, Harding joined the front row saying,

'Right, you blow the whistle and I'll show you how to scrummage.'

With the ball heeled against the head, Harding emerged from the scrum, grabbed the whistle and instructed the prop forward to play on.

A finer example of Harding's efficiency as a referee emerged in a match between Butleigh and Taunton Police. Harding disciplined the police back row concerning the offside once too often. The police open side wing-forward heatedly announced to Harding,

'That's it. I've had enough. I can't stand it anymore. I'm sending myself off.' With this he wheeled around and to Butleigh's delight marched towards the touchline.

Harding knew that without some wise counsel and guidance, and at least a modicum of formality, the exuberance of the founding body might be dissipated in a lost cause. The organisation of fixtures had worked surprisingly well considering that, as Harding recalls,

'Nobody selected or announced Butleigh's team; anyone could play if they turned up. Nobody bothered too much about the referee. Anyone would do. Nobody bothered with showers they simply went to the pub covered in sweat. Nobody bothered with food as the pub usually came up with something. Nobody bothered to tell the newspaper, the result was unimportant anyway. Nobody bothered when the opposition failed to arrive. Sometimes fixtures were invented to ensure a convivial day's drinking. In fact nobody bothered too much about anything. As long as there was a match of sorts then everyone was happy.'

'But there had,' he continued, 'out of necessity to be some formality. For technical and legal reasons, the club needed to be part of the county structure. The main point for this affiliation was participation the players' injury insurance scheme operated by the Rugby Football Union. This was essential for the wellbeing of any unfortunate who might suffer a serious injury while playing. What the club wanted, as every club that has ever existed wanted, was to ensure that these duties were efficiently performed. What was needed was a traditional 'boring old fart' to administrate in a low key and to say the magic word 'no' when the wildest schemes were suggested. Every other club had one, the county had one and Twickenham had 59 of them. The system worked, so Butleigh needed one too.'

Of course what the club needed - quite significantly - was someone to pay the annual insurance premium. Harding, a man of honour, fulfilled this duty at the beginning of each season. To repay the debt an empty gallon demijohn with 'Ball Fund' written on it was placed at one end of the Rose and Portcullis bar which Harding used to raid at regular intervals in an endeavour to recover his outlay. His next task was to write to the Somerset RFU to declare he had taken on the role as secretary.

'I would like you to consider that the administration is at last in responsible hands.'

Harding was thus rewarded with a demand from the Somerset RFU requesting a copy of the club's accounts. There were no accounts. There was no treasurer so Harding took on another role. He became treasurer and created Butleigh's first set of accounts. With no record of any expenditure, and with his only certain knowledge being that the credit column was that nearest to the window, he created a document which included expenditures such as the compulsory insurance and the affiliation fee. For good measure 'nil returns' were made to illustrate the nature of the club. These included the purchase of balls (someone's girlfriend had a father high up in Gilberts), and line whitener (acquired from the Millfield ground staff). Ground rental was declared as peppercorn. To balance this, an income was needed so this was itemised under one heading as 'Whip rounds, raffles, money left in the jar on the bar'. These brief details of income and expenditure were submitted and, later, an official letter was received complaining there was no sign of an audit. Would Butleigh please re-submit proper accounts?

Diplomacy was called for. Harding arranged for the Somerset secretary (a bank manager) to visit the club when over a beer it was pointed out that the production of accounts was quite inappropriate for a club that did not need them. There was no membership fee. Life membership was free. There were no rates, no building maintenance, no bar, no transport costs, no gas, no electricity, no water (there was a cattle trough), no catering, basically nothing. The County Secretary was happy and, to his glorious and everlasting memory, he declared Butleigh to be an account free club. His next task was to 'modify the nonsense submitted to the Somerset handbook'. This was considered by some to be his first backward step as Butleigh's secretary. Before things became regulated, the allocation of tickets to Twickenham had been generous because Butleigh had appeared to be one of Somerset's larger clubs.

'At first glance,' says Harding, 'the handbook entry implied the club had numerous teams playing at all levels. Spoof names of celebrities were included in all sorts of prominent offices. A 'Miss Cynthia Payne', a well known hostess of doubtful virtue was listed as social secretary. Mr 'Dago Agostini', a car designer, was responsible for mini rugby. There were coaches, a trainer, a club physician, a youth development officer, treasurer, welfare officer, all with fictitious names and unobtainable phone numbers. The prank had to end and it soon did.' The true officers were listed and the ground location was given accurately – by the co-ordinates of longitude and latitude; 51 degrees, 5 feet N and 2 degrees, 40 feet W. For further accuracy this was later changed to the Ordnance Survey.

One of the great attributes of rugby clubs is the camaraderie between players and teams. Butleigh were no different, however things were happening that were not being formally recognised. The secretary found to his horror that sometimes the most wonderful exchange tours, for example those with the two Spanish clubs, CAR (Club Amigos del Rugby, Seville) and CRAP (Club Rugby Athletico de Portuense, Puerto de Santa Maria) were not officially documented with the authorities over here. If they were not approved by the RFU they would be no players' insurance. Approval was a mere formality requiring just one form to be completed.

This was highlighted with the unscheduled visit of the Jockey Club de Argentina. On a three week, six match rugby tour of Europe they decided they would like to play a match in England and they would like to visit Twickenham. They had played Puerto, Butleigh's old rivals in Spain and Puerto recommended Butleigh. To Butleigh's astonishment they found that they were to be the Argentinian side's only match in this country. The game was arranged on the assumption that the tour was officially acknowledged but it turned out that this was not the case and, as a result, a reprimand was received from the president of the Somerset RFU who had checked with the proper authorities.

Hastily arranged at a few days notice a Friday afternoon match, a team of farmers and the unemployed were organised for a 1pm kick off. The president of the Somerset RFU Fred Ellison was invited to watch. Arriving in good time at Butleigh's ground in Kingweston the county president was surprised to see no evidence of the two teams. Butleigh, having met at the Rose and Portcullis at midday, arrived at the ground at 1pm, changed and waited patiently before a phone call informed Butleigh chairman Tony Berkeley that the Argentinians had become traffic bound leaving London and were still an hour and a half away. To a man Butleigh left the field jumped in their cars and drove off.

'Well,' said the county president, 'your lads seem to have taken it quite badly. I suppose that match is forfeited.'

'Nonsense,' replied Harding, 'they've all gone back to the pub.

Berkeley meanwhile drove down to the A303 dual carriageway some five miles away and awaited the tourist's coach in a lay-by, throwing a rugby ball up into the air at oncoming coaches to attract the driver's attention. An hour and several pints later, in the Rose and Portcullis, scrum half and captain for the day Jerry Morse led the first strains of singing. Singing before a match is often an ominous sign that the game would not necessarily go Butleigh's way. After a further half hour a phone call from Berkeley indicated that the Argentinian coach was on its way to the ground. Butleigh lost by thirty-four points to twelve.

The Argentinian experience of Butleigh's facilities was invigorated by the local Barton St David showers, specially hired for the occasion but not as rewarding as anticipated since no-one had remembered to light the boiler. Cold showers for all; an aspect of the game to be discovered for the first time by the poor Argentinians used to a warm climate. It was freezing and they were not amused. For the first half hour after their Spartan experience, they remained silent and huddled in a corner. Then food arrived; hospitality prevailed and by closing time the frost barrier had been crossed, the language barrier broken and warm-hearted friendship prevailed. The Argentinians swore everlasting devotion to the joys of coarse rugby and retuned to their hotel wiser and happier for their experience. Luckily no-one was injured.

Harding recalls, 'Butleigh RFC made its mark on the rugby world when they protested at having to sign the RFU 'pledge of compliance to amateurism' in 1994 on the grounds that the RFU was amateur anyway. Insistence that they sign again in 1995 led to further protest and also to the name change - Butleigh Amateur Rugby Union Football Club, with the emphasis on 'amateur' and 'union football'. Approval of this must have been one of the last acts of retiring RFU Secretary Dudley Wood thus making Butleigh the only Amateur Rugby Union club in the world.'

Chris Harding.

Throughout the saga of 'professionalism' there have been examples of injustice. The 'grass-roots teams', have sometimes been treated indifferently. Butleigh was a victim of Twickenham tyranny. It was the wish of the Somerset RFU that every club in the county should become affiliated directly to the England RFU. Butleigh finally complied with what was really a compulsory directive from the county authority. Butleigh now had a vote at national level. Out of curiosity Harding attended a full AGM of the RFU where the matters of the game were conducted quite properly in the presence of the press. However, as the matter of professionalism progressed over the years it was seen that the professional body was determined to gain control by removing the franchise from the non league clubs in the game. Within six years Butleigh were down graded to 'associate level' with no voting powers or voice. Butleigh felt betrayed by the game they so faithfully supported.

Evidence came of this when the Yorkshire Constabulary in the form of the Humberside police visited Butleigh for a weekend tour. The fixture came about when Butleigh lock forward Harry Buckle's engineering van was broken into when he was working in Humberside. Whilst discussing the loss of equipment the subject of rugby came up. A few months later a coach of Yorkshire policemen pulled into the Kingweston Park. Following an early visit to Roger Wilkin's cider farm, they enjoyed a commendably upbeat weekend. Most were young and fit dual Union and Rugby League players and a discussion developed regarding a reciprocal tour back in Yorkshire. Butleigh were to go north and try their hand at rugby union on the Saturday and rugby league on the Sunday. There was only one doubt on the secretary's mind - player insurance. However, as the leading rugby union club, Bath, at the time had recently played a similar series with the leading rugby league club (Wigan), there were hopes that two of the most humble clubs in the country could enjoy a similar experience. Harding wrote to Twickenham asking permission to play a League match and to enquire whether the player insurance would be valid. The reply was disappointing – the answer NO. This in spite of the fact that the two leading clubs in each code had recently done so; it was one rule for the wealthy clubs and another for the poor.

The secretary's role seemed unstoppable. Harding recalls, 'When England played Ireland in Dublin in 2005 the national anthems were sung as usual before the match. For the English, the lead singer sang the wrong words to the British anthem. The third and final lines were sung as 'God save OUR Queen,' not as they should be 'God save THE Queen.' Preposterous!'

He wrote to Francis Baron, chief executive of the RFU to explain the faux pas. Baron's protective secretary intercepted the message, writing back that it was a matter for the Irish and complaints should be sent to Dublin. Harding responded by sending an email to every county and constituent body's secretary explaining the situation. He also sent a copy to a well known, retired civil servant of some standing, who replied that he too had noticed the mistaken words. Strangely enough, the very next day, a letter was received from Twickenham admitting the error. As a reward, the civil servant became the first and only recipient to be awarded honorary life membership of the club. Harding also wrote to that well known amateur rugby enthusiast the (then) Deputy speaker of the House of Commons who had also noticed the errors and who also agreed. Another letter was sent to the head of Protocol at Buckingham Palace expressing concern for her Majesty's feelings. A reply was received from the Royal Household thanking him for his concern stating that Twickenham would be advised to do things properly in future.

This of course was the last thing that the chief Executive of the RFU, the beleaguered Francis Baron, needed. England had just lost their third Six Nations match in a row and possibly one of the last distractions needed at that time was a barrage of advice concerning how accurately the players and entourage sang the National Anthem. The letter received from Twickenham admitted that the Butleigh secretary was right after all, saying that in future Twickenham would ensure the correct words were sung both at home and abroad. England went on to win their last two matches against Italy and Scotland.

President – Tony Berkeley

One of the great boosts to Butleigh was the arrival in 1978 of England's youngest Maritime Merchant Seaman Captain, Tony Berkeley. He had not only played for a club which at the time was in the forefront of English Club

Rugby, but, whilst spending months at sea he had taught himself to play the guitar. From Buddy Holly to Wild Rover to 'That was a terrible song', he could seemingly strum anything. He could also drink anyone to their knees whilst happily playing on. Such was his popularity that farewell parties would be arranged prior to his four month's sojourns to sea and many more on his return. Stories that Tony would bring back were the thing of legend – including his tale of the Hector Heron.

'After an epic four and a half day journey from Stansted to Singapore in a four engine 'barn' I eventually managed to join the majestic 'Hector Heron', an ex whale oil tanker, which languished, akin to a beached whale, in Keppel dry dock. I had been banished to this marine colander by my previous captain who had taken great exception to my incinerating cockroaches with lighter fuel.

'Climbing the starboard gangway during a general refit, I was greeted by the chief engineer who was taking on board delivery of vast quantities of new brass and copper bits from the local chandler. These bits appeared to be then traversing the vessel before disappearing down the port gangway where the second engineer was frantically tallying their scrap value with a representative from the same chandlery.

'We're raising money for the new four lane scalectrix racing game', the engineer explained. 'We've been saving up for hours'.

'The ship eventually sailed from Singapore for the Arabian Gulf to load 35,000 tons of diesel for the Mobil terminal in Sydney, Australia. The events that took place during the following weeks can only be described as hectic. A stabbing, one suicide, six engine breakdowns, a mutiny and the discovery of a stowaway - a parrot who was promptly named Archie after the first engineer.

'The mutiny among the Hong Kong Chinese crew occurred just south of the Persian Gulf when the Scottish second engineer was the unwilling recipient of an affectionate approach from one of the Chinese crew. The Scotsman responded, somewhat ungallantly, with an iron bar across the head of his suitor - there was blood everywhere. A maritime riot ensued causing the captain to radio for assistance from a Royal Navy destroyer which dispatched half a dozen completely mad marines to rectify matters. Members of the crew were arrested and returned to Hong Kong leaving the tanker to be manned by the officers entrusting myself as junior cadet to peel potatoes and prepare the cooking.

'Sailing out to Australia through the Antipodean answer to the Bay of Biscay a huge storm ripped into the vessel taking away most of the catwalk, pipe work and crucially, unknown to the officers, jamming the forward anchors. Our orders were changed at the last minute.

'Don't go to Sydney; go to Fiji in order to sign up a replacement crew' - very precise nautical instructions.

'A few days later we duly arrived off the Port of Suava to be greeted by the harbour pilot, his wife and children, a representative from the consul and various dignitaries. This visit, reflecting the first occasion that a Fijian crew was to be operating under a vessel flying the Red Ensign, was evidently a matter of great pride and occasion to the Island. Approaching the harbour and new wooden jetty we could clearly see a large military band, fully dressed in white uniforms and wearing pith helmets, being conducted by a stout fellow in full regalia. An immense crowd had gathered.

'Let go of the starboard anchor', boomed the pilot with great importance gilding his voice. The Chief Officer released the brake on the cable drum connected to the anchor store. Silence ensued. Where there should have been a metallic chattering charge of link and iron, there was silence.

'No go, Sir,' muttered the officer on the forecastle deck. 'It's stuck in the pipe.'

'Let go the port anchor!' shouted the now anxious pilot. A second lever was thrust forward. Nothing happened.

'It's stuck as well,' shouted the officer, visibly shaken, meandering backwards.

'The Hector Heron tanker, complete with its 35,000 ton volatile cargo, hit the jetty to the band's strains of 'Rule Britannia' at no more than four knots. The primarily wooden structure gently splintered, generously accommodating the ship's bow. The splendid band, eyes like saucers, possibly unfamiliar with the discipline of modern day docking procedures kept a sense of dignity in the testing circumstances wavering only slightly on the rippled apron. The dynamic arrival of the tanker had, however, generated enough vibration to loosen the eight ton port anchor which, crucially, the Chief Officer in a moment's distraction had forgotten to put back on brake. The anchor, now released, plummeted forty feet landing on, and continuing through, the last portion of unscathed jetty. Momentarily the crashing anchor upstaged and out thundered the musical fanfare some ten metres to the right and it fell only just behind the traumatised conductor for whom this dramatic first world greeting was proving quite irresistible'.

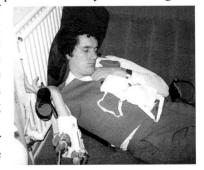

All in all it was a wonderful time for a young cadet; an ideal grounding for the extraordinary eccentricities of Butleigh Amateurs RFC. Tony's seagoing experience stood him in good stead at a later date. On tour in Puerto he was called to account for the antics of some of the Butleigh team aboard a ferry.

Puerto 1994 - the lifeboat incident

Back at the hotel, preparations were nicely underway for the biannual Guadalajara swimming race. This significant sporting event is competitive in that the object, apart from winning, is to survive the ordeal. An incident of drowning would not be a surprise. Wing forward Paul Panton once struck out on a previously un-charted course to shore, only to discover and swim through with ever-weakening strokes, raw sewage from an outlet pipe feeding directly into the sea. This is one of Spain's endearing features, especially in the warmer months, an evocative bottom-of-the-garden, outside-bathroom, stale and gassy odour.

Fatty Edwards was busy assembling his group of triads for the ferry trip to Cadiz, Moose, Letchie, Tim Gelfs – all for one and one for all. It's important for security and peace of mind 'on tour' to form yourself into a group that pledges complete trust within itself – to buy each other drinks, to ensure a safe arrival home in a taxi if an evening turns unexpectedly emotional, to protect rooms from pillage and, most important, to wreak vengeance on any person or group that threatens disruption or concern.

Cadiz is one of Spain's more historic cities, featuring strongly in European history and of significant architectural interest to visitors. However, despite numerous visits by Butleigh over the years, no group of players has been able to report with accuracy any details of this magnificent place, beyond the merits of two splendid bars within the immediate vicinity of the ferry terminal.

Eight hours later, having prepared for the race in their own particular style, the swimmers re-boarded the ferry for the two mile journey back to Puerto. As the ferry chugged gently out of the harbour, Tim Gelfs possibly mindful of the events ahead realised that life boat drill, an absolute must in these circumstances, had not been observed and also that in Latin countries the procedure might be a little rusty. Halfway back across the channel with the boat's captain showing no apparent interest in this vital safety procedure, Gelfs expertly executed the rope tackle release mechanism thus launching the life raft, a curious, large, wooden box-shaped affair into the sea with a loud and satisfying splash. Captain Jose Gonzales cursed violently and rallied his crew and boat into a change of direction in pursuit of the rescue craft, bobbing happily in its recently found freedom. However this sudden action proved unrewarding for, rather as a cat may chase its tail, Captain Gonzales initially failed to appreciate that Gelfs had retained possession of the end of the long rope tethered to the slightly distant but now pursuing craft.

Red faced and blowing with indignation the captain roared for an explanation.

'This man is totally crazy . . . loco,' responded Tony Berkeley rather unnecessarily. 'There is always one,' he continued as he tried to placate the furious captain.

The captain's eyes bulged with fury as the rescue craft was finally rescued followed closely by a further distraction as another loud splash was heard to starboard. One of the passengers had thrown himself overboard.

'Oh no,' Berkeley shouted, 'not again.'

Then turning back to the totally enraged captain, 'Two crazy people, we have two.'

'I'm sorry it's just an isolated suicide attempt it's just….'

He broke off, interrupted by the sound of another body hitting the water and then two more. The captain spun round and raced, half stumbled up the short stairway to the deck panicking that at this rate of exodus there would be no passengers left to ferry.

Berkeley stayed still, lowered his head and sighed. How was it, after more years than he cared to remember piloting and sailing 100,000 tonne merchant ships around the world, that he was now being held responsible for losing control of a large ferry and tourists? Captain Jose Gonzales on a different level was asking similar questions of himself. Returning to his cabin he picked up the radio handset. Berkeley, lighting another cigarette was aware, as 'Policia, Policia, por favour' was summoned up, that an interesting evening lay ahead.

Stepping off the ferry, Berkeley entered a local hostelry to be greeted by the whole tour party including those who had elected to jump ship. They were soaked, standing in large pools of Guadalajara possibly tetanus infected water.

Berkeley after the harrowing ordeal with the ferry captain ordered a well deserved beer and was just about to take a first draught when he felt a tap on his shoulder. Turning round he found a diminutive chap in denim jacket and jeans. 'Policia' he announced, revealing a large revolver.

'Good afternoon, officer, what's the problem?' Tony responded having also noticed a large police contingent surrounding the bar.

'Some of your peoples are being stupid,' he said.

'Well that narrows it down to about thirty,' thought Berkeley.

'They are jumping from the boat into the river,' and, he continued, 'I need to know who are these peoples.'

The puddles around the culprits had by now almost reached the doorway. Berkeley chanced his luck, 'The gentlemen boarded the ferry, paid for a return ticket but decided to leave earlier. While it may be stupid it cannot be deemed illegal as they were fare paying passengers not stowaways.'

This logic flummoxed the officer who accepted Berkeley's offer of a large beer and an apology. It was the start of an excellent relationship with the Policia Locale, many of whom were to play for Butleigh in future tours. The Spanish, you appreciate, are brilliant. They understand the ways of life and therefore it is the only place we can take (safely-ish) the Colonel – Ian Saunders – and the rest of Butleigh Rugby club.

Berkeley's skills had to come into play when dealing with another potentially difficult situation whilst on tour in Puerto in 1992. To understand how this came about, it's important to know a little about another Butleigh character.

'Colonel' Ian Mustard.

His first game for Butleigh was Minehead Barbarians away in 1989. Uncannily the police became involved. Never malicious - always a gentleman, always 'a misunderstanding', but always at some stage of the greater days, a police presence was summoned for assistance.

Butleigh left the Rose and Portcullis one morning with a van full of players and supporters sitting on straw bales in the back, and headed off to Minehead via Street to pick up prop forward/winger Paul Lockyer. Despite waiting, as always, for ten minutes outside Lockyer's house whilst he completed his Sunday morning emotional experience, for once he really couldn't travel. This was something for which he paid dearly twelve hours later.

When the team arrived at Minehead, Greg Cox, Chubby Weare, Elliot Davis, Eddie Teagle and Ian Saunders, all usually Wells rugby club players were waiting patiently for them. Minehead Rugby Club was one of the popular clubs to visit, not only for its immense after match hospitality, but because the twenty four miles of road to Taunton seem to have a never ending number of popular pubs. On the return journey, a visit to a Kentucky Fry restaurant was requested. By now everything seemed an attractive proposition, including the purchase of flashing headbands at £1.99 each. Unfortunately, wing forward Paul Panton decided his orange squash was of dubious quality and launched it backwards, high in the air over his shoulders.The police arrived within fifteen minutes. Carnage, including a vast array of chicken drumsticks and wings lay scattered across the restaurant. The Colonel – no fault of his – had been in the thick of the fight. Tidying up with brooms and dustpans Butleigh moved on to another hostelry before, somewhere around midnight, arriving back at Lockyer's house in Street.

All the straw which had been forced into the front of the van, despite a furious defence by the front seat passengers, was dumped on Lockyer's front lawn to pay him back for not travelling with his team. Arriving at the Rose and Portcullis, players and supporters disembarked and the captain made his way back home to his family. Creeping into the house, that within a few years he was quite appropriately requested to leave, he placed the multi-coloured flashing head bands on each of his three daughters' bedsteads as thoughtful presents and then climbed quietly into bed. Screams from the girl's bedrooms an hour later alerted his long suffering wife that something was terrifying the children. Green, red, orange and blue lights circumnavigated the ceiling and she was horrified when she saw the state of the bedroom completely strewn with dust and straw.

Saunders finest hours were yet to come. On tour in Puerto in 1992 the Colonel was with a group of friends taking the early evening air they passed a house, the front door of which was open. Seizing the opportunity, the others pushed Elliot Davis through the doorway and pulled it shut. Shouts and hammering on the inside of the self-locked door turned to worse as a woman descended the stairs to confront her intruder. 'Knife, she's got a knife,' screamed Davis. The colonel charged the door, splintering it open. The woman, now convinced it was gang robbery on an international scale, lunged at the colonel who picked himself up and, running for his life, charged down the street pursued by the knife wielding hysterical Senora.

Looking for an escape route the colonel rounded a corner and, with the woman commendably close at hand, spotted a busy Burger Bar. Without hesitation he threw himself through the serving hatch. In the furore cutlery, plates and condiments cascaded noisily and the mustard pot which Saunders

It wasn't my fault.... had landed on exploded. As tour organiser Tony Berkeley explained, 'I'd enjoyed a lovely evening with my Spanish friends and having returned at 2am had just fallen asleep when my hotel room phone rang. It was the owner of the hotel.'

'Tony – allo – Tony.'

'Yes Manuei,' 'Tony there is a problemo.' 'One of your peoples is being very stupid. The Policia have brought him here for his passport.'

Berkeley, heaving a sigh, lit a cigarette and taking the lift down to the foyer was greeted by Saunders in handcuffs flanked by two Policia. But what really took Berkeley's attention was that the colonel's shirt was smothered in bright vivid yellow mustard. 'What's happened Colonel?' inquired Berkeley.

'Tony, it wasn't my fault, it's a big misunderstanding.'

Over the years the Colonel a fine, belligerent Rugby player on the field caused further mayhem. Returning from a night out at daybreak, with his great farming companion Kimberley Gane and waiting to order a taxi, he asked to borrow a mobile phone from someone setting up their market day stall. Not only did the stall holder refuse but so did his compatriots. The Colonel as a consequence set about the market traders stands,

Tony Berkeley in The President's Waistcoat.

36

charging belligerently, bravely into each stall until someone let him use their phone. The market was set back an hour whilst the Policia were contacted to resolve the problem.

On another occasion, returning late, he spied a 'taxi'. Jumping in he ordered the driver to take him to his hotel – 'pronto!' The police car into which he had jumped, most obligingly drove him to his destination before producing handcuffs and demanding to see his passport. On the 2006 tour to South Africa, showing that after decades the tide had possibly turned, a police patrol car pulled up alongside the Colonel. It was late at night and the police, who were from outside the area, asked if he could possibly give them directions to the nearest Police Station.

Berkeley's President's waistcoat was evidently a hard won item of clothing and one of which he is justly proud.

Fixture Secretary – Andy Nixon
Andy, a former Swanage and Wareham tight head prop, arrived at neighbouring farming village, South Barrow, in the late 1990's. With his previous club he had won Five County Cup Finals.

Running out for a number of local clubs it was Butleigh that suited the dairy farmer's outlook. Before many games had passed, Nixon's reputation as a destroyer of opposition ball carriers became established. Forwards making the error of running straight with the ball were not only heavily battered in full stride but pummelled directly backwards before, if they were really unlucky, being driven, buried into the turf by the eighteen stone impact. A sequence of shuddering hits brings alarm to the opposition and cheers from Butleigh. To be Nixon-ed is to be flattened with a resonant crater-ing crump rippling across the pitch. The victim often displays a temporary state of paralysis suffering ongoing physical and psychological damage. Nixon's party trick is to arrive as the opposition ball carrier straightens his run, picking up speed at the pace of a head down, warring bison involved in a territorial dispute. Picture a large granite boulder on the end of a thick wire hauser demolishing a disused northern factory. Casualties within his own team are not unknown. To appreciate the kind of pain threshold suffered, stroll to the end of any driveway and sprint, accelerating into a closed garage door.

Nixon contributes a few words on New Zealand rugby.

'New Zealand is losing the plot. Appreciate their last years of world competitiveness as the end of an era is in sight. Their farmers are selling up – mainly to the Dutch workaholic dairy industry – and their bright, intelligent, young women are fleeing a workaholic society for profitable employment in Europe. In Auckland, bedrock of Kiwi rugby, a professional football team has just recently formed. New Zealand while being a terrific nation of people is a generation behind in certain aspects of culture.

'A farmer, for instance, involved in a useful game of cards will phone home instructing his wife to milk the cows and make sure they are put in the correct paddock while checking his supper is in good order. Towns often consist of little more than a garage which also sells chainsaws, outboard motors and lawn mowers. There is a pub where the farmers spend much of their day, and a hardware shop that includes paints, electric fencing wire and shotgun shells.

'A shop stocking Fischer and Pikes, the leaders in Pacific Rim Domestic appliances, is considered the ultimate seduction when farmers are courting, especially if it recently opened a coffee franchise within. So it is only ten miles down a gravel track through a couple of fjords – when not in flood – to a well stocked ironmongers where the women folk can enjoy a cup of coffee while waiting for their men to emerge from the pub – irresistible. Within twenty years unless their national side can snaffle up leading Southern Island players from Fiji, Tonga and Samoa their national side will be delighted to beat Portugal.'

Nixon also has something to say about League rugby.

'On April 7th 2003 the Somerset RFU met at Wells rugby club to discuss in particular the falling number of players from this great game. The conclusion reached was that many young people now work on a Saturday and are unable to play, while clubbing all night is often considered a sport in itself. Butleigh conclude that for many, league rugby has become a second job in itself. Also for players it is the changing face of employment that has had greater effect. Many of the great players of the 1970's and 80's were farmers - John Jefferies, Ben Clarke, Graham Dawe, Bobby Weir, Peter Winterbottom; builders, Mike Teague; policemen, Paul Ackford, Martin Bayfield, Dean Richards; the armed forces, Tim Rodber; doctors, Jon Webb, JPR Williams and the city brigade, Simon Halliday.

'Nowadays, and this filters right down to grass root rugby, there has been an astonishing decline of manual workers on farms with the police no longer encouraged towards rugby. The professional services are being taken over by women displacing men into house husbands often spotted exchanging coupons with others outside schools at collection time. The answer will be, if it's financially viable, a prospering professional premiership with continuing decline in playing numbers among junior sides. Many will and have expired, Cheddar and Blagdon locally. Some will amalgamate, Nailsea and Backwell. Westlands and Yeovil became Ivel Barbarians. However there is one exception - a continuing expansion of non league sides who play midweek and Sundays, who involve families, play for fun, exist on a shoestring and are allowed to develop their own style of rugby fixtures enjoying the very best of times within the finest and most honourable sport in the world.'

Home Run

Following an away match against Rampisham, Butleigh players were sitting in the Talbot Inn. In one corner of the room a television was showing the Arsenal vs. Aston Villa match in which Arsenal defender Lee Dixon scythed down a Villa attacker conceding a penalty. This prompted Andy Nixon to comment, 'Strewth, I used to go to school with Lee Dixon. We used to beat him up on the way home.'

The penalty taker lined up for the shot, ran in, struck the ball and goalkeeper, David Seaman, made a brilliant save.

'You did what?' we asked.

'Yes, we used to beat Dicko up on the school train on the way home.' said Nixon. 'He was only fifth choice to get into the school team. You'd never have thought he would play at this level, let alone pick up forty plus caps for England. His father used to play for Manchester City and made

Dicko practice time after time. He'd take him down the club and force him, literally force him into becoming a top grade footballing defender.'

'But what about the school train incidents?'

'Oh, that was only a bit of fun on the way home,' explained Nixon. 'Ten of us would cram into a compartment and scrap until only one of us was left inside. It was the Secondary Modern lads versus the Grammar School. That was just the warm up. The train would arrive at Wilmslow Central which is where the real fun started. Another train full of kids from the Handforth Estate would come in. The estate had quite a reputation. The police would never go in after dark and in daylight they would only go in in pairs. These kids were something else. Their train would arrive with lads hanging on for dear life by their fingertips on the outside of the carriage. As soon as they landed on the platform, missiles would be hurled at our lot, stones, bricks and cans, then they would run over the bridge because everyone had to leave by the same turnstile. Every day there would be fights and the station staff were at their wits' end. They would sling open the gates – it was a stampede, mayhem. In the build up to November 5th, it was a re-enactment of World War 2, fireworks thrown everywhere.'

In this kind of competitive environment it was no wonder that Lee Dixon became a hardnosed, uncompromising international defender and Andy, who didn't take up rugby until he was twenty eight, made the Swanage and Wareham first team within a few weeks of joining the club.

4. Pig Rugby

Which pig to follow...?

'Late 1950's in the Sudan,' Charlie Wrighton related, taking several draughts of his favoured real ale Doombar. 'We used to play a game of rugby on Christmas Day; Officers vs. NCOs, a hell of an occasion. A few drinks beforehand the troops would line the pitch and instead of using a ball we used a greased piglet; needed to fence the pitch off to keep the blighter in play; hell of a job to maintain any continuity; damn things kept slithering their way out of loose scrums.'

Questioned about the state of the pitch the former captain said,

'Damned hard, with sand, stones and rocks but that wasn't the worst of it. The sappers had mined the pitch with thunder flashes and smoke bombs. A pack down on the wrong spots and the scrummage would disappear in a cloud of cordite. It was a monumental experience. Afterwards the officers and the sergeants would prepare and serve the troops their Christmas meal.'

'What about the piglet?' someone inquired.

'Oh it always won the day, always got away, that's why we needed at least six to complete the match.'

'A whole litter then?' reasoned livestock farmer Tim Gelfs, captain of Dorset and Wilts newest club Rampisham RFC. 'I think', Gelfs continued, his eyes flashing with enthusiasm, 'that this tradition could stand re-enacting. When's Rampishams home fixture with Butleigh?'

This of course is very much the amateurs' role in the professional era - to keep the past alive. There would be the inevitable animal rights protests along with 'piglets for rearing not rugby' placards; however, there was no doubt, after the Sunday match and following several pints of the Red Lion's excellent real ale, which way the proposed match fixture with Rampisham was going.

'Of course we'll need a hardy breed of pig,' said Farmer Gelfs, face alive with excitement, 'I reckon a Gloucester Old Spot or a Tamworth. They're pretty fierce.'

Five months later -

At midnight, the night before the match, a tractor churned noisily into life within the quiet, idyllic village of Rampisham. Twelve hours to kick off; Gelfs, having spent a long evening with his team in the Talbot Inn, planning and scheming tactics for the following day's pig rugby match against visitors Butleigh, had returned unsteadily on foot to his farm and found, to his horror, on checking the piglets that they were missing, escaped, leaving an empty pen behind. Gelfs dashed to the farm tractor, started it up and roared off into the dark night in pursuit. A mile down the road Gelfs swerved violently across the road having as near as dammit run over one of the piglets.

'It was why I took the tractor,' explained Gelfs, 'a car wouldn't have been up to it.' Retrieving the tractor from the large hole it had created in a neighbours' hedge, and with the pigs recently sighted, he set off once more.

'I finally rounded them up, but I was really pleased as, in the chase, I glanced down at the speedometer and clocked them doing eighteen miles an hour.'

The next day, after a late breakfast, Gelfs examined the piglets and they were still fast asleep, snoring peacefully after their midnight bid for freedom. Little did they know quite how the day would unfold. Rumours of the age and size of the animals had been causing Butleigh concern. For instance, no-one was sure how Gelf's plan to hold a piglet show the day before the match, with rosettes from first to sixth place in order to recruit the best piglets, would go. Another rumour was that the piglets were well-grown boars and had been coached to charge, savage and gore a Butleigh multi-coloured shirt filled with pignuts.

The two piglets - Margo, the (female) gilt, and Gerry, the (male) boar - had, after the previous night's exertions, slept particularly late and well. Apart from a ten minutes interruption over a lighter than usual breakfast of milk slop and rolled barley (pig muesli) they snored serenely away in their pigsty.

By two o'clock, in contrast, at Rampisham's Talbot Inn the two rugby sides were warming nicely to the match ahead. The home team's head grounds-man Scott Critchell was relating how pleased he was with the outcome of his line-marking machine efforts using a John Deare 30-6000 pulling a five furrow reversible plough. By shortening the top linkage system Critchell had engaged just the front furrow to plough in order to gouge out twelve by eighteen inch touch lines around the pitch. Angle irons, clad with wooden stakes, made for rugby posts. Red bailer twine, loosely slung, indicated crossbars. Following further refreshments, the teams eased themselves out of the Talbot and down a country lane to the changing rooms – a large open barn at Farmer Gelfs' farmyard situated amongst tractors, trailers and carelessly strewn feed bins one of which was a large black plastic silo filled with freezing water and a long handled broom posing as the after match washing facilities. Mulled wine was served to maintain the teams' buoyant expectancy.

Meanwhile a tractor and trailer had set off to collect the four legged rugby balls.

The two piglets, with sleep still in their minds, oinked and grunted begrudgingly as they were herded up into the trailer for the trip to Rampisham's rugby pitch. At the ground a large, well-wrapped village crowd on a blustery cold day complete with press photographer and local dignitaries, sensed with anticipation an unusual event of sporting spectacle ahead.

A large tub of reduced goose fat, held over from Christmas, sat near the middle of the pitch with a small gathering of children giggling excitedly around, sleeves rolled up to elbows awaiting the unloading of the pigs. The Rampisham captain lowered the ramp of the trailer to the ground and guided Margo and Jerry onto the pitch. Until then the pigs had shown no more than an idle interest in proceedings, however, moments later their eyes opened wide, as big as saucers, as the throng of happy shouting children thrust their hands into the bucket of fat and commenced smothering the pigs in grease. The strong-smelling, glutinous grease possibly confirmed the pigs' misgivings.

Match referee Tony Berkeley then blew his whistle, a silver-plated French hunting horn, for the teams to come together for the toss up and the match commenced. With a further blast of the horn, and a scrum-down on the halfway line, each side's scrum half introduced a pig into either side of the melee. It was the last moment at which the official was to make any figment of sense out of the match.

Berkeley remembers that, 'After moments of grunts and snuffling the pigs reappeared at the base of the scrums and, obviously sensing freedom, took off in opposite directions up the pitch pursued by two sets of forwards with a bemused three quarter line unsure of the next move. If ever there was a requirement for more than one official on the pitch, this was it. I didn't know which pig or which set of forwards to follow.'

The gilt was the more purposeful of the two pigs and, sensing home, she scurried at great pace towards the village end try line. Upon entering the twenty two, three Butleigh players caught up with her and picking her up attempted to run back up the field but, so unnerving was the squealing, they promptly dropped her before she head butted her way through a weak tackle giving the hapless tackler a painful raking (trottering) as she slithered free. Momentarily slowed by all this attention, Margo was then caught by a more experienced Rampisham farmer. In a classic pig-hauling manoeuvre she was upended on her back and hauled several yards before Butleigh forward James Timms tackled the Rampisham farmer causing him to release Margo who was promptly swept off her feet and carried the last ten yards to the Butleigh try line for the first score of the match.

Some distance away frantic blasts of the horn by referee Berkeley indicated an infringement of the laws of the day by the other pig who had not only run off the field of play but, despite some desperate defence, had made his way through a thick hedge and was being pursued by a number of the fitter forwards across an adjoining field.

Rampisham won the match by 10 (two pig tries) – Andrew and David Vickery, to Butleigh's 7 - James Timms (one converted pig try). After the match, with the pigs safely returned to their pen and the players severely but effectively washed down in the bath of freezing cold water as well as with a one thousand pressure per square inch water jet, the teams returned to the Talbot Inn.

'Basically the problem was that the boar was stupid - thick as s***'. Gelfs, the Rampisham captain, summed up. 'He didn't seem to grasp the fundamentals of pig rugby in that you have to stay on the pitch,' he continued, 'but Margo, the gilt, was an absolute natural, great lines of running, loved the rucks and mauls and seemed genuinely thrilled when she was finally carried over the Butleigh try line for the first score of the match.'

Gelfs, eyes glinting and with a pint of Worthington in his hand, was holding court in Rampisham's Talbot Inn about the future role of pigs in rugby. 'The ECI might give the rugby club a grant. They've already issued guidelines for including toys in the rearing pens to prevent boredom and cannibalism – why shouldn't they encourage pig rugby?'

Three years later, Gelf's plan for the ultimate breed of pigs for rugby has produced some intriguing results. Margo, after her convincing display, was saved for breeding. She has just produced her third litter of piglets. Whereas in her prime rugby days she weighed just over eighty pounds, now she weighs over four hundred. She is quite magnificent; it would take a whole set of forwards to lift her up. She scrummages a heavy, corrugated metal pig hut around her paddock and she has found love to fulfil Gelf's desire to breed a race of super rugby pigs. She has fallen for Boris, an all black wild boar from Wales who, although only a half of her size, has somehow consummated their relationship and is the father of a most exciting recent litter of piglets.

5. Other Clubs, Players and Rivals

The Pulteney Arms Bath

Bath landlord, Terry Nash, at the still legendary Pulteney Arms, ran a rugby side that other social rugby sides could only dream of. It was a side full of current International, County and Bath first team players together with more than useful recruits from the many Bath regional clubs. It wasn't specifically designed to be an outrageously useful side, it was just that top players mixed socially with other rugby players and they all enjoyed a pint in the Pulteney Arms. The Pulteney Arms even merited a mention in the England vs. Wales match day programme as being the other team that fly-half John Palmer played for.

Bath Civil Service wing-forward Hallsey suggested to landlord Nash that Butleigh might be the ideal place for the Pulteney Rugby Club to visit. Within weeks, the day after a triumphant Somerset County fixture against Yorkshire which had been decided by a disputed drop goal awarded late on at Bridgwater and Albion's ground, a coach pulled into the Rose and Portcullis and crates of cider were purchased. The bus, containing amongst others such eminent players as John Palmer, Simon Jones, Dave Trick and Jon Hall then carried on to Butleigh's home ground.

In a grand gesture of hospitality, Butleigh scored three tries before a rapid nine try blitz from the visitors redressed the balance. Despite John Palmer losing a front tooth in a line out while playing out of position at wing-forward it was a most sociable day. The Rose and Portcullis closed at 4pm and the teams moved down to No. 3 Compton Street where a wild party erupted during which Butleigh centre Robert Laver disappeared upstairs with a lively, flirtatious young lady.

Dreams and challenges abounded. One of the Pulteney team's characters, Tucker, was not a Bath player but he was a leading force in social entertainment. Late one evening he accepted a £50 wager that he could not, given some assistance, para-glide the length of Bath's Westgate Street. This was a five hundred metre, reasonably straight, lightly housed boulevard.

Early in the morning, a car complete with a tow hitch stood waiting, engine ticking over, at one end of the street. A long length of coiled rope lay primed adjacent to a partially prepared para glider. A police car on patrol then eased around the T junction slowing to a stop by the small group of aerial entrepreneurs. 'Good day lads, what exactly are you doing?' enquired one of the officers.

'Sailing, sir,' replied Tucker, 'we are packing the sails to go sailing, leaving first thing tomorrow.'

The car moved quietly on. The group breathed a collective sigh of relief

and continued their preparations. The rope was now tethered to the car's tow bar stretching some thirty metres back to the triangular para-glider with Tucker, like a sheep in the talons of a magnificent eagle, harnessed ready to accept the £50 challenge. The car, engine revving, eased forward taking the strain. Tucker, supporting the light para-glider frame on his shoulders, walked forward. The car accelerated. Tucker jogged then ran. A whirr of revs, a drop in engine note as the tension of the rope kicked back, a change of gear, lightness in Tucker's feet then, dramatically, he was ten feet off the ground, rushing past hedges, gateways, and gardens. Although moving forward and up, Tucker precariously perched, realised his direction was no longer on a perfect course but drifting perilously towards a building.

Bouncing off Pontin's Garden Centre roof with the tow car braking, Tucker fought valiantly to control his descent into a nearby car park. To his good fortune, his fall was broken by slamming onto the roof of a parked car. Stunned, Tucker thought the end had come as darkness settled in a fluttering sensation over his head, but it was the para-glider canopy that had arrived engulfing him a moment later. This is how he was found by the Police.

Later at The Island Club run by Roger Spurrell, the Bath Rugby Club Captain, Tucker, bruised but unbowed, presented his para-glider to the cloakroom attendant. She refused to offer a ticket for it and Tucker was concerned by this casual approach. 'How will you know which one is mine?' he complained.

Tucker not only took a month to fully recover but at the end of it was £10 down. Initially sued for something akin to assault and battery, Tucker was eventually found guilty of trespass and fined £60.

A further challenge that resulted from playing the Pulteney Arms was that, whilst the winners received the Lougi Taverna shield, the losers were presented with and required to drive home an unlicensed wreck, with no M.O.T, whose rear seats and boot were filled with horse manure.Butleigh were once the recipients of this disaster. The club entrusted their well-girthed prop forward, Kenny Everett, despite the fact that he was emotionally tired and had little driving experience, to chaperone the excitable seventeen year old Mad Marcus Stock who had flourished his recently acquired provisional license. Estimating that there was at least half a gallon of fuel on board the desperate trip was cheered off, pursued by a small convoy of excited followers. This turned into an unsteady pub crawl with the eager group laying odds on where and when the luck of the intrepid duo would run out.

Rumbridge Pack away
One of the legendary sides of the eighties, the Rumbridge Pack at Eastleigh, near Southampton played at the Trojans RFC. There were shades of the Pulteney Arms about the quality of the side and many county players turned out for them. One of their players, fifty nine year old Swanage and Wareham lock forward Ralf Breeds, currently plays for Butleigh.

Presided over by millionaire philanthropist, Allan Grant, Rumbridge enjoyed wonderful overseas rugby tours. These would last for three weeks. In 1979, taking a minimum of fifty players, Rumbridge visited St Lucia in the Caribbean. The club returned with stories of endeavour, mis-understandings and with a five year ban from going back.

Among the tourists was eighteen year old prop forward, John Collier, a fresh faced cockney not only on his first rugby tour but in possession of his first Visa card.

By the end of the three weeks he was delighted to have negotiated an increase on his £300 limit to just under £2000. Eventually he wrote a number of furiously indignant letters to the Bank involved, complaining bitterly when they demanded repayment and telling them how irresponsible they had been to issue a credit card with that sort of scope for his first trip abroad.

Young Mr Collier's tour got off to an immediate start on landing in St Lucia, where with the help of colleagues, he hired a Land Rover and roared off into the jungle in search of refreshments. Three days later, having occupied and somewhat dominated a rural hostelry, they set off in their doomed hire vehicle and attempted to rejoin the rest of the touring party based some miles away in a comfortable hotel.

Appearing at pace, the Land Rover, ignoring the niceties of the hotel car park, shot up over the front steps into the foyer through the general reception area scattering guests and residents aside. It made a brief appearance on the manicured lawns before accelerating on and into the hotel's previously much admired swimming pool.

Following a sustained period of aggrieved unrest on the part of the hotel management, a breakdown service involving a small crane and a powerful winch finally proved up to the Herculean task of hauling the stricken 4x4 back to the garage. Here the intrepid John Collier explained how, whilst driving through the outback, a native boy had hurled a coconut through the

windscreen of the Land Rover causing him to swerve off the track and into an irrigation canal. Not only was this explanation accepted but to Collier's disbelief, another Land Rover was duly made available for further hire.

Appearing at pace...

The Campaign for Real Ale Rugby

This campaign is a vital piece of amateur rugby union development. A popular Public House selling Real Ales is approached requesting a fixture. Butleigh organises the chosen pub's home team, complete with a set of occasionally washed shirts, (still on loan some three and a half years later from the local rugby club), a ball and referee. All the landlord has to do is allow access to the flag stone floor, real ale and a nearby field. The game, thirty minutes each way maximum, is played usually on grassland. White line marking out is an optional extra – hedges and stonewalls often suffice. (See Rifleman's RFC away regarding electric fencing). An informal timetable is agreed – 'Whatever you do, don't come back while we are serving Sunday lunches.' The occasion, especially the after match celebrations, can be anticipated knowing the drinks and settings will be exemplary. Reports on two excellent examples of such matches follow.

Red Lion Babcary 5
Butleigh Amateur 25 or 26

In a thrilling, pulsating end-to-end encounter, watched by a good natured Sunday afternoon crowd and a bemused flock of recently displaced sheep, the Amateurs eventually wore down a stubborn Red Lion defence to emerge victorious by 25 or 26 points to 5. The curious double score line reflected different interpretations of the laws of the days rugby match for, similar to the schism in early Christianity, rugby players harbour deeply polarised views on the conversion. The origin of this local difficulty lay in heavy rainfall in Babcary during late October which had left the sports field where the match was scheduled to take place under several inches of water.

The fixture was rescued by local farmer, George Kingsdon, who offered three nearby fields for choice of pitch. The first one, rather narrow, was laced with outcrops of rusty barbed wire, the second boasted a vibrant yield of thistles but the third, an ancient cider apple orchard, looked promising. Apart from a handful of old tree stumps on the potential playing area there were two useful trees, set some ninety metres apart, still bearing fruit, which might indicate the uprights. Farmer Kingsdon, Babcary Rugby Club head grounds-man, adeptly removed the offending tree stumps with his JCB digger in the minutes before kick off. With a blackthorn hedge as one boundary and a winding stream as the other the match kicked off in the early afternoon following beers and mulled wine.

Red Lion Babcary vs Butleigh.

Before the match there had been some concern over the structural stability of the changing rooms but the landlord insisted the condemned sign was, despite the somewhat dilapidated appearance of the eighteenth century barn, a joke and had nothing to do with the South Somerset Health and Safety office.

Prior to kick off it was agreed (and it was this decision that led to the final inconclusive score line) that to convert a try or penalty the ball would have to be kicked and lodged into the branches of the acting upright -a tree at either end of the pitch. A slight complication arose in the pre-match gathering in the Red Lion bar in that a triumvirate of referees had arrived to officiate at this historic encounter. One, Tony Berkeley, thoughtfully agreed to remain in the bar while the other two, a Millfield School teacher Simon

Wynne and local developer Fatty Edwards, agreed to share the responsibilities and referee one half of the pitch each.

When Butleigh fly-half Trigger Macnab was kicking for a try conversion his attempt lodged in a tree - but the wrong one. His ball had sailed over the relevant apple tree, bounced once in a nearby lane and up and into a poplar tree growing in boundary woodland. So impressed was referee Edwards that he awarded one point for effort, however referee Wynne took the orthodox view of no point at all. Following the match the alfresco showers rigged up by Mr Kingston in the pub garden were supplied by a hosepipe from the kitchen via a watering can into a modesty cubicle comprised of slatted blue pallets.

25 or 26?

The Rifleman's Arms 15
Butleigh Amateurs 15

The Rifleman's Arms with its low wooden ceiling is a smoky, dimly-lit hostelry in Glastonbury where businessmen, builders and convivial locals mix with roll ups, real ales and rough cider to a background of reverberating Hendrix, Pink Floyd, Dylan and Meat Loaf classics. This is the real bar at the end of the universe and all forms of galactic life may be found there.

Rife's landlord at the time, former Millfield prodigy Ivan Garrett, occupied one evening in the questionable sensible company of the Butleigh captain, finally agreed by closing time that, together with a number of Tor's more colourful players who drank there and with a few of his regulars, he would be able to raise a side to play Butleigh. Waking the next morning Garrett, believing he had probably dreamed the proposal, thought nothing more of it until he read in the local paper that the Rife's would be playing Butleigh following three days of consecutive rain in April.

Outside the rain fell and the forecast was dismal. A pitch was needed and smallholder Pip Curry agreed that the Rife's could use the bottom meadow which was suitably flat and situated on the far side of Glastonbury Tor. He would move his Welsh cob 'Paddy' off the field and the teams could use the horse's stable to change in. The only snag was that there was a large, reed pond in the middle of the field. Garrett realised that this might be to the home team's advantage and, in order to foil Butleigh's renowned organisational abilities, he immediately accepted the offer and contacted the Butleigh club. 'We've got a pitch, Berkeley can referee and, looking at the forecast, we'll play you on Friday, meeting here from midday.'

'That's early for a Friday. What time's kick-off?'

There was a pause, and then, 'As the light begins to fade,' Garrett reasoned, 'we shouldn't have too long a second half.'

Three days later, by 6pm, the Rifleman's Arms was packed to the gunnels – as busy as the landlord had ever known it - with pints of the good stuff, yards of ale and flagons of cider being consumed with gusto. The jukebox hammered out 60's classics, singing was in the air and referee Berkeley was taking questions and large ports, bribes from both teams. Kit bags, shirts, muddy boots and some Wellingtons were piled high in corners. On the bar, tipped on one side, lay a mask and snorkel.

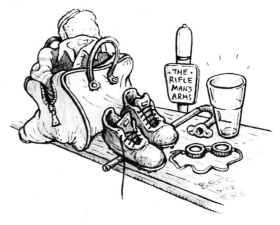

By 7pm the fixture was in the balance. Fatty Edwards had sung two songs and was beginning a search for a large metal tray to accompany his third. He had already eyed-up a carelessly dressed young thing as his 'Allouetta'. With that, Referee Berkeley eased his way through the bar, circumnavigating a number of players and a chair that wasn't there, to take the light. Scudding clouds across a setting sun had indicated possible fading light. The bar hushed, the clouds drifted by releasing sunlight once more across the Somerset levels.

'Fill 'em up again lads,' he announced to an accolade of cheers.

Ten minutes later, standing purposefully in the foyer, 'Right – there's no doubting it. The light's beginning to fade, time to make a move.'

Within minutes a convoy of vehicles, some untaxed, many battered, spluttered like a spitfire squadron into smoky life before being eased gently out of the pub car park turning right onto the main Shepton Mallet road out of Glastonbury. A mile down the road a left hand turn was attempted taking the snake-like convoy down the one and half mile winding, hedge-lined lane towards Wick and the Home team's ground. Arriving some minutes later outside the Wick Holiday Farm Caravan site the vehicles pulled over on to the nearside verge, setting back the early show of daffodils previously standing there so proudly.

Players jumped out and walked across to a rusted, five-bar gate, its hinges loose in their sockets. Leaning on the gate, players stared down the long, steep grassy and mud-packed field to a distant meadow. A lone horse stopped its evening grazing, raised its head and stared back. In the middle of the field a large, reed pond beckoned. Right then, nothing in rugby ever felt so promising as the prospect of what the next hour might have to offer.

Having changed in the nearby stable, and with the pre-match, mulled wine heated and distributed, the teams set off down the hill. The horse was moved to the next field. The pitch bore no white lines of any description. Boundaries were afforded by a well-established blackthorn hedge on the far side, a length of ticking electric fence on this side and two sets of seven-foot, rusty lengths of angle iron thrust into the soft peat-like turf some ninety metres apart.

The Rifleman's XV, in clever, dusk-defying white shirts, lost the toss. Butleigh elected to kick off. Butleigh fly half Dai Roberts kicked off the game with a deft slow hanging kick that landed in the middle of the pond followed, a split second later, by the diving Butleigh tight head prop forward who belly flopped only yards from the ball followed by his loyal pack. The

Rifleman forwards led by Tom Harding landed moments later. For a full thirty seconds there was no more rugby. Spectators strained their eyes but apart from a great deal of activity within the pond there appeared little sight of the ball.

The problem lay in the physical effect that the condition of the pitch was having on the forwards. The consequence of landing in the icy-cold reed pond, the bottom of which was a soft, treacly, stench-ridden bog, was to leave the players involved almost paralysed. The confused activity seen by the supporters was, regardless of the whereabouts of the ball, the action of players trying to extricate themselves from a potential drowning incident. No one had ever played on a pitch so demanding. It was going to take some adjusting to.

Progress however suddenly developed as Rifleman's lock forward Steve Sturgess, a six foot five Hells Angel Biker from Shepton Mallet, emerged from the pond clutching the ball. With mud, slime and algae cascading off his body he set sail, arms and legs pumping, for the Butleigh line. Sturgess was wearing a Hannibal Lector type brown leather mask. This horror movie vision of the occult fended off three slithery half-hearted tackles to score the Rife's first try. Undoubtedly the home teams' most intimidating player, his immense presence was reduced from that of a marauding, dungeon enforcer to that of a domesticated lap cat by engaging in a half time roll-up with a group of his biker friends who had come along to support.

First try for the Amateurs was scored by press photographer, Jason Bryant, who showed a startling turn of pace to touch down between the posts. Mark Baggelaar, sports editor of the local *Central Somerset Gazette*, was heroic in defence (dislocated knee cap, torn shoulder ligaments) whereas sports reporter, Jon Ryder (full back) stood behind the safety of the rugby posts, in a pair of Wellingtons, sipping cider before retiring at half time.

As the light begins to fade...

51

Further first-half tries for the Rifleman's were scored by the gap-toothed gypsy Christian Hall and winger James Eagle before Constable Matthew Slade touched down for Butleigh. At half time refreshments were served from a portable bar. Rifleman's full back Nathaniel of Wessex reported that he had never attempted sport in such darkness. Following the restart, action could only be followed by tracking shouts of encouragement and curses. As the referee later confessed,

'I thought the game refereed itself quite well, anyway but by the start of the second half I'd lost sight of the ball and most of the players.'

Ten minutes into this half a terrible protracted crunch echoed across the moor land turf as Rifleman's scorer James Eagle, having missed an all encompassing tackle, hurtled into the far touchline hedge allowing Butleigh's Trigger MacNab to level matters with the final play of the match.

The Butleigh captain, near exhaustion, sitting in darkness happily shivering in the stench-riddled, muddy pond towards the end of the game, reflected how the next match in a week's time, would be played in baking sunshine in Spain, thirty degrees centigrade of heat on a bone hard pitch in Marbella.

Proving how hazardous rugby can be even after the final whistle, Butleigh second half full back, former veteran speedway ace Ken Hawker, became entangled in the darkness with the live electric fence causing him to display a noticeable facial tick for the rest of the evening. Back at the pub showers consisted of a hosepipe through the kitchen window onto the patio before players and spectators alike packed into the Rife's where celebrations and singing went on till the light began to dawn.

North Wootton RFC

Created out of Butleigh, with a little prompting by youthful Millfield Junior School teacher, Chris English, and charismatic free spirited scrum half, James Phillips, Butleigh's sister club North Wootton evolved in 1996.

Former Bradford and Bingley 1st team full back, James Foggy Phillips, charms the players and he persuades them to turn out. Chairman Chris English adds structure by finding a whistle and a ball for the match days and handling complaints, of which there are potentially many, from opposition sides and the Somerset RFU. The Wootton club is a fast, open playing class act. They struggled in the early days to field a competitive front row but are now more comfortable as, through age and a willing attendance at the bar, key players are putting on much needed weight. The team gains much from the character of Phillips who, with an engaging smile, black, curly, tousled hair and eyes a fraction bloodshot, always has kisses for the girls and handshakes for the team..

'All right? How are you?' Wherever Phillips goes there is an upsurge in handshaking. When he arrives, when he leaves, greeting the opposition, during the match, at the end of the game, coming into the pub, leaving the pub – always the hand shakes. This is the usual conversation on arrival.

'What's going on? Where is everyone? Are you alright – what a mess – it's all my fault – no, you're right, you really are – where's Brooking? – I'm sorry we're late – it's an absolute shambles.' He laughs, lights a cigarette, accepts a hot mulled wine.

'Thanks, that's really good of you. Are you sure? Have we got enough?'

He then changes into his kit, rambles, half jogs onto the pitch where, upon the start of the match, he proceeds to launch vast passes in the direction of his team mates.

Butleigh and North Wootton just before kick off.

As the game progresses Phillips zigzags a lot, apologises a lot.

'Sorry Matt, sorry that pass was awful.' And with the game very much in the balance or having gifted the opposition another intercepted pass he suddenly ups his game and, on playing well enough to inspire England, scores a try and makes four more, poaching the game from under the visitors' noses. At the final whistle more apologies. 'I was terrible, really shocking – shouldn't have stayed out so late. Thanks for playing – you were really good.'

Cavalier, laid back, gifted. The most entertaining of scrum halves always laughing, an absolute gentleman, a nightmare for the opposition, a brilliant player for Butleigh Rugby Club, always with an endless queue of top totty girl friends, he has been known at kick off time on a Sunday to call a friend in a hushed voice.

'Will, Will, is that you? Will, I feel awful, can you help, where am I? I'm in this flat somewhere.' Then, lowering his voice, 'What's her name – the girl I'm staying with – what's her name, can you remember? Can you come over? Are we playing today? What time's kick off? Can you pick me up?'

Out of this ongoing mayhem, this next generation sister club to Butleigh was founded – exactly the same ideals, playing occasional matches on a Sunday, hit and run long weekends to Ireland, annual visits to Yorkshire, Somerset Cup matches or any team that offered a game. North Wootton's home team pitch is a piece of land too wet to farm on, offered by one of their players, farmer Jeremy Hayles. Christened 'Hayles Bog', this superb quagmire of a pitch was often too wet to take white emulsion paint lines, so a local supermarket in Wells offering a 'buy one get one free' offer on self raising flour would be visited. Chris English would purchase thirty plus bags to mark the pitch, cutting open one corner of the bags and tipping the flour to mark up the lines where a particularly tenacious lawn mower had mown away the bog related grasses until the petrol had run out.

The changing rooms were located on the farmer's dairy farm up a few stone hewn steps into an old hay loft where dusty bales of hay accompanied stored furniture and a sofa. An old wind up 78 gramophone sat on one side providing echoes of Butleigh's early cup match days. A dead bird (a song thrush) lay on the wooden boarded floor and to one side a large, hard plastic, faded blue, children's paddling pool later to be filled with hot water from the dairy as the after game washing down facility. Outside a 2000 PSI water blaster, normally involved in washing down the cow yard, was turned onto players to assist in removing some of the more tenacious mud clogging clay stuck as glue on the heads of the forwards. North Wootton plays on the heaviest pitch in Somerset and Butleigh, made up of farmers and builders, has a pitch as wide and fast as an aerodrome.

Phillips has learned well from his years with Butleigh, for instance when it comes to Cup matches he organises his team two to three days before the match. For tours to Yorkshire it's a full week before leaving. It matters not one iota whether there are seven or seventeen on the bus. Everyone has four or five pints before leaving two hours late on the five hour journey up north. The coach hammers up the motorway and everyone brings a sixteen pack of the strongest lager. Loo stops are avoided, instead half gallon empty squash containers are filled and tipped out of the back windows of the bus. If you can encourage the windscreen wipers of the car behind to start up it's an extra cheer. A huge social group of old school friends meet up that night when extra players are drafted in for the match.

On one occasion the tourists played Ilkley and headed off there via the Cow and Calf and more lashings of Tetley's bitter. Arriving at the ground, Ilkley had no idea North Wootton were playing them. 'You can't play our firsts; they're in a league match. Our 3rd XV are playing North Ribblesdale and they've been here for twenty minutes.'

Phillips had a word with the 3rd XV captains.

'Right, they've agreed to play us after they've had twenty minutes each way against each other. Then we play Ilkley for thirty minutes then Ribblesdale for thirty minutes.' An hour and a half later, with two wins under Wootton's belt, it was off to the bar preparing for the next day's match against a Bradford and Bingley XV who did know we were coming.

Phillips lives for the moment, the present, the happening right now. As a player he thinks no more of kicking the ball into touch to finish or tighten up a match than twenty stone Butleigh full back Steadfast would attempt to clear his line with a kick. Tournaments, cup matches, international clashes playing for either Butleigh or Wootton even if leading by a bare point still, nail bitingly, sees Phillips on his try line throwing huge reckless, brilliant passes to anyone to keep the game alive, to keep frantic opposition in with a chance, not slamming the door of match winning opportunity in their face; making the very best of that moment to keep the excitement alive.

Butleigh Amateur RUFC 38
Blake's Bears 31

At the Amateur's home pitch in Kingweston, on October 3rd 2003, preparations for the day's events were in disarray. The water heating dynamometer had blown several vital gaskets so that cold water running direct from the Wessex Water mains into and out of the friction heating machine remained freezing cold.

Winger Mark Edgar volunteered to drive to near by Barton St David's sports field in the hope that a home team fixture there, would allow their excellent hot showers to become available. Edgar's luck held, a hockey match was going on and they gave Butleigh permission to use the facilities. Three hours later Edgar's luck turned and he had to purchase Butleigh a free round of drinks to compensate for the showers being as icy as the water in the Amateurs washing trough – no one had put money in the meter.

Back at the pitch, with the 12 o'clock kick off approaching, there were just five Butleigh players present of whom one, Stuart Vickery, brought news of dead arm unavailability. However, two pieces of good fortune had visited the Amateur's situation. Firstly the pre-match mulled wine was coming nicely to simmering point and secondly, the opposition had failed to materialise.

Butleigh winger Tim Gelfs arrived and brought news of livestock developments. The wellbeing of the eight mice which had been used in Easter Monday's mouse racing, fund raising epic at the Barton Inn was causing concern. Following an unfortunate incident involving the farm cat, there had been a recent crisis among the remaining three mice. Not only had there been a thorough disagreement but one had died and another had eaten it leaving only a pile of bones neatly stacked in one corner of the cage. Blake's Bears than arrived in sprightly form, only fifteen minutes after the agreed time of kick off. With Butleigh up to nine players and two of the visitor's cars still in search of the ground, the mulled wine was served. Within half an hour there was such an atmosphere of conviviality that the kettle was refilled and another offering brewed up. Finally, with skipper for the day Trigger MacNab prised out of his passion wagon, the two teams strolled onto the slightly rabbit warrened pitch and commenced the match.

Blake's Bears, who were celebrating their tenth anniversary year accompanying a first success in the Somerset Cup (courtesy of a bye in the first round), quickly ran up a two try lead. Butleigh full back, twenty stone Joseph Steadfast Smythe initially found the visitors three quarters elusive. However the tide turned as Bears punted a high, long ball into Butleigh's 22 which, when collected by Steadfast, caused much alarm amongst the previously all conquering visitors. Steadfast considers a defensive kick into touch both demeaning and cowardly. His charm is to gather the ball and charge shoulder down, battering as many would be assailants as he is able to hunt down, in a somewhat erratic path out of defence.

Steadfast, whose preparation for an extended night of romance is to prepare himself via a vigorous loofering in the shower beforehand, achieved a full time body count of 24 batterings, conceding just five tries and three conversions in the process. Also known as Jody Stead, this man is another vivid personality familiar to Tor RFC as well as to Butleigh.

Joseph Steadfast-Smythe

Members of the top echelon of rugby players are usually quoted as revealing great athletic prowess in their early years. Lock forwards were often excellent basket ball players, legendary full back JPR Williams was an outstanding junior tennis player, wingers were often schoolboy sprint champions. Then there was 'Jody Stead' who showed potential of a different kind – providing a startling vision of what gifts he might bring to the world of rugby by the tale he had to tell an enthralled audience at the Rose and Portcullis.

'When I was fifteen,' said Steadfast, 'I used to go round to this mate of mine's house on a Saturday evening and, I couldn't believe it, there was his Dad stretched out naked on the living room floor in front of the fire with a two litre bottle of red wine. He used to have this Rotweiller, loyal as anything; soon as you approached the old man he'd give a low growl. If you moved back he'd settle down and start cleaning himself, you know what dogs are like, nothing's ignored. When he'd finished he'd start on the old man, give him a good clean as well. You've never seen anything like it. Anyway, once the old man had dozed off my mate would sneak off, grab a wedge out of an upstairs drawer, take the keys to his Dad's 3.5 top of the range coupe and drive us to a Bristol night club. My mate wasn't that tall, had to sit on a cushion to see over the steering wheel.'

'The secret was,' continued Steadfast, 'to drive right up outside the night club door so the bouncers and any talent could see the flash car and then they'd let us in. Only fifteen, it was incredible and the women we used to pull. Then at the end of the night my mate on top form would drive us all home.'

With this display of precocity Steadfast was always going to play for Butleigh however in the intervening years he became National Aerobic champion and for one season captain of the hugely progressive local Saturday team - Tor Rugby Club. He could also dance, which in his position as a tight head prop, an increasingly large tight head prop, was mesmerising since he combines a style of Caribbean rhythm meets break dance hop. With Butleigh he would, in the early years, turn up when ready, crack open a lager and watch from the sidelines, freeing more lagers, before venturing on the pitch not as a twenty stone forward but in his preferred position as a non-kicking last line of defence, attacking full back.

Steadfast enters a team, The Mighty Ducks, in the Magnificent 7s. Each team that enters establishes their own camp area. Some muster straw bales, some bring their own tent, some set up tables and chairs with sun brollies for shade. Steadfast brings a family sized swimming pool. This is inflated, filled with water via a hose from the clubhouse and bottles of cider and lager are carefully arranged. This practical scheme not only keeps the drinks cool but the entire Mighty Ducks squad climb in and sit down, only emerging to play their matches on the pitch before returning hot and breathless to the calm of their own small marina.

Cup Rugby

Some two years after Butleigh's first games with the Plume of Feathers an extraordinary envelope appeared at the Rose and Portcullis Inn. The pub was a natural sorting office for the regulars. Gossip and invitations were shared, bets could be placed on horses, one night stands were arranged and drink-enhanced pathways to ambitious dreams opened up, brightly lit as a fun fair.

The extraordinary letter informed Butleigh that they had drawn Taunton Rugby Club away in the first round of the county cup competition. Whilst delighted with a further addition to the fixture list, to this day no one is sure as to how we were either involved in the cup competition let alone suddenly

Butleigh vs Taunton, 1st half.

a member of the Somerset Rugby Football Union. The game was a magnificently contested affair, with Butleigh losing 24 – 12, although we put out a particularly useful side including Fenners, Frith, the Reid brothers, Shed Jackson and Rob Laver. Despite defeat, Butleigh gained the better of the second half score-wise. Something unique was created that day and following a few after match beers at Taunton (and singing) a phone call to Geoff Hicks at the Rose and Portcullis persuaded him to open an hour early. There on the flagstone floor beer was downed and the team formed a huge circle and arm over arm, sang and celebrated a fantastic performance against one of the county's better sides.

Over the following ten years Butleigh awaited with increasing trepidation the arrival of the Somerset envelope with news of the draw, hoping upon hope for a home draw. It never materialised; for ten years the cup draw was always away, always against one of the stronger teams in the county; Old Reds away – cup winners; Combe Down away – two years running; Weston Hornets and Oldfield old boys. As a number of our players were cup-tied to other clubs it meant that the main priority was fielding a team for the occasion. Anyone that could stand up would be drafted in.

Against the Weston Hornets two Spanish students on holiday and with no rugby experience were drafted into the outside centre and wing positions. This lack of practical experience was balanced by two Welsh forwards working at a Glastonbury building site RN Navy and P.E. Narth. 'Narth' played 1st team for Penarth rugby club but, helpfully, was serving a 3 month ban for GBH on the pitch. As a tight head prop and mobile with aggression he gave a prodigious performance in the forwards, at one stage running half the width of the pitch and pole axing a Hornet's forward with a delightfully maiming, thundering, late tackle. A howling gale lashing down the length of the pitch keeping the score to just 16 – 0 to the home team in the first half. Sadly, despite suggestions to the referee, ends were changed at half time.

Oldfield Old boys away was another torrid event. However, by now Butleigh had learned to make more of the day. Full back Stephen Gillam brought his 78 wind up record player into the concrete bunker visitor's changing room and played a stirring version of Chilli Pompeii to the team in the minutes before kick off. The effect was however somewhat lost by the thunderous noise of the home team's studs hammering on the concrete floor accompanied by booming shouts and barely veiled threats. The referee meanwhile offered Butleigh a glimpse of hope in that moment before the match from hell. Inspecting Butleigh's boots he dramatically pronounced thirteen of the team to have illegal studs on their boots.

'You'll have to change your studs. You can't play in those they haven't got a safety kite mark stamped on them.' Spirits were lifting in anticipation of an abandoned match but he continued, 'I will, however, ask Oldfield if they will accept the risk.'

Butleigh vs Taunton, 2st half.

A momentary halt in the home team's thunderously blood curdling preparation next door raised Butleigh's hopes only for them to be dashed again, 'Its okay lads, Oldfield are prepared to accept the risk – the match is on.' At half time with Butleigh a number of scores down the day's efforts were rewarded by Butleigh's magnificent supporter, Murray Eaglesome, dressed in a black tie ensemble bringing champagne on a silver salver with champagne glasses to ease the torrid encounter.

A turning point in cup fixtures was the brilliant Fatty Edwards letter to the Somerset RFU cup committee lamenting the fact that his club, Aller, had been forced into playing two cup matches two days running; both away games. He suggested that it would be fairer to grade the draw so that early rounds would be played against similarly gifted sides. As a result of this suggestion the cup matches were thereafter arranged so that, in the early rounds, like clubs played like. Butleigh's cup successes then flourished with some positive results each season. In 1999-2000 Butleigh had four match cup wins, including one over Tor Rugby Club, before losing at home in a close encounter with Oldfield Old boys.

In 1982 Butleigh were due to play Backwell away and full back Stephen Gillam, over a beer in the Rose and Portcullis, cleverly suggested that we should spend a Saturday afternoon watching Backwell play, assess them and see where their strengths and potential weaknesses might lie. Having never been to Backwell the captain and the full back met in the Barton Inn for a pre trip couple of pints asking legendary landlord Phil Cabble, who had heard of Backwell, how best it would be to drive there. The landlord produced a dusty AA road atlas and the two set off along with the captain's 3 year old daughter Julia strapped in a baby chair in the middle of the bench seat in a white Toyota van. Heading up over the Mendips despite consultations with the map the scouting party became lost – not only that, it was now 3pm and the match had kicked off half and hour ago. Driving down a high edged, narrow country lane, with time for accurate assessment of the team diminishing, they came across a large flock of sheep in the road. Not only this, Julia made a significant request for her potty. Producing the required item, the captain stepped out of the van and positioned his daughter over the said receptacle. It occurred to him, with sheep bleating in the rear, just how challenging scouting the opposition could be.

The trio arrived at Backwell for the last ten minutes of the match. The players on both sides looked jaded with fatigue and it was only in the clubhouse after the match that it transpired they had been watching the 2XV teams. The following week's cup match away was tied ten all at half time but with Butleigh number 8 Robin Reid, eyes blazing, threatening to deck anyone who missed a tackle the game was secured in the second half.

Tor Rugby Club
The Saturday side at Tor RFC in Glastonbury was formed in the early fifties as a breakaway side from Wells RFC and originally the side was strong; Gareth Edwards turned out occasionally and also Charlie Hannaford along with a number of gifted players including Millfield teachers. The club's fortunes ebbed somewhat when that generation retired. However, under various inspired captains, Jerry Morse, Geoff Calder, John Marshfield, Malcolm Dykes and Paul Lockyer, to name but a few, the club played increasingly improved rugby. A truly outstanding committee was formed including Brian Harbinson (now president), Tim Kelly, Otton, Bruce Williams, Mark Edwards and Keith and Pat Elver. They have gone from strength to strength with this sound leadership and the mighty club has expanded through the judicious use of grants and fundraising. The club has

Butleigh vs Tor

now moved to new premises with a sophisticated two storey clubhouse. Many former members still remember the wooden hut at Beckery with great affection recalling the antics that took place there. However, the roof fell into disrepair and it became awkward when rain that poured in had to be re-routed through an open window via plastic sheeting.

Tor is now one of the more successful sides, both playing and financial, in Somerset. It has become a magnificent success, with social functions taking place almost every week, and it is a club that should progress to become one of the top in the county. Many Butleigh players have played at Tor on Saturdays, Sundays and recently midweek. The more rugby you play the better and fitter you become. Playing in a promotions battle in recent years Tor played unbeaten Bristol Harlequins as the last league match of the season. Eighteen hours after many of the Tor 1st team had played for Butleigh vs Riflemans, they played their best rugby of the year to take this match; a Tor team laced with Butleigh and North Wootton players; all for one, one for all, the greatest rugby days of our lives.

Jock Green

Jock's a proper Scotsman; you know, barely intelligible when sober, completely incomprehensible after six pints, talk the legs off a chair - incidents of misunderstanding abound. He is a loose head prop, five feet ten high, five feet eight wide, thick set and solid, red flushed face, full head of grey wire brush hair, large nose, close-set eyes, immensely gregarious – his own man. Captain 2nd XV and, the first game of the season, Bath Civil Service Club away, had been won 60 – 12. Everything had gone so well for Jock Green in his first game.

The rest of his team decided to test his character in time of adversity and when disappearing to the loo at the Slabhouse Inn on the Mendips the rest of his team did a runner. Despite a desperate sprint after the last remaining van with the tailgate open he was left on the Mendips twelve miles from home. In a state of fury, he ripped open the car door of an innocent pub leaver and demanded a lift. He arrived in Wells and went on a search of pubs before taking a taxi back to his home team's clubhouse in Glastonbury where more drama ensued as he found himself with less than two pounds to pay a five pound bill. His wallet had been typically left in a team mate's car upon the visit to the Slabhouse Inn. Fully on the rampage, determined to discipline his errant team Jock borrowed some cash, downed a sequence of beers and whiskies and headed off to nearby Street. Recognising the lead singer of a Blues Rock Band playing there, he rushed in, picked up a speaker and threatened to launch it into the band if they didn't reveal the whereabouts of his team.

An even more intriguing situation occurred during a visit to Totnes Rugby club in Devon; a friendly 1st XV fixture so far away that a coach was hired for the day. Following a close result, and several agreeable hours, Tor went on a tour of local hostelries in Totnes ending up in exuberant form in a pub where they began helping themselves to bottles of wine thoughtfully displayed in an ice basket at the end of the bar. However, it was another incident that finally convinced the landlord, who was originally delighted with the twenty strong visitation, that all was not well. It started when Jock Green became disorientated while searching for the toilets.

As Jock Green's long suffering and immensely patient wife Heather would agree, following nights such as these their bedroom at home would be better served by en-suite facilities than the old stand-by of the wardrobe. Jock, by now desperate for the men's, found a quiet darkened room in the pub and proceeded to relieve himself in one corner.

Following the incident the visitors' rugby coach left Totnes under a full police escort, at twenty miles an hour, blue lights flashing with a decree not to return to the licensed premises ever again. The problem lay not so much in the unfortunate choice of room for Jocky to relieve himself as the presence of the pubs sleeping Alsatian guard dog curled up in a safe corner of the room.

'I swear ah ne'er saw the creature,' lamented Jock. 'It woke up in a frenzy, ah near lost everything.'

However, non-smoking Jock Green's gift for misunderstanding reached premiership levels years later when Jock borrowed a friend's new car, without his knowledge – he was away – to engage in a dash to Calais on a booze trip to stock up on essential refreshments. Stopped on the return leg of the journey by the Dover Customs officers they were unimpressed by the 20,000 cigarettes and one hundred litres of wines and spirits noticeably weighing down the borrowed car. With merciless authority, not only were all the spirits and cigarettes confiscated, but, the car was impounded leaving Jock making frantic arrangements for a lift.

'How do you expect me to get home?' he desperately asked the officer.

'There is a bus stop beside the Dock's gates.' was the reply.

6. Where is everyone?

Kick-off for matches on a Sunday morning is timed like this – meet at eleven thirty, mulled wine served from eleven forty-five, kick-off twelve midday. This (apart from cup games) never happens. Matches kick off between an hour and an hour and a half late. The problem is that if you advertised a match to begin at 1.30pm it wouldn't kick off till 3pm – if at all. Players become desperately fickle around opening time and once into their second or third pint often stay where they are. It's crucial to arrange a kick-off when they are still carrying the full effect of the morning hangover from the night before, that is before they actually feel like a drink.

This, of course, is why fifty plus phone calls or texts are needed to guarantee a minimum twenty five players that inevitably whittle down to between twelve and seventeen on the day. When Butleigh are at home, the opposition invariably arrives first. In the pre mulled wine era the Butleigh captain would only start marking the pitch out twenty minutes before agreed kick-off, and he always marked out the nearside touchline to the club house first knowing that the opposition's arrival was imminent. As soon as a convoy of cars or the visitor's coach arrived the tactic was to accelerate away from the visiting party, briskly marking out a try line, and then to commence work on the markings of the far side touchline and five yards line out. If you were white lining anywhere on the nearside someone from the opposition would inevitably wander over to ask where Butleigh were. If however you were eighty metres away marking out distant far side touchlines you didn't get bothered. The far side of the pitch is also an excellent vantage point from which to watch for any sign of the Butleigh team arriving. A healthy clue is six or seven Butleigh players in evidence at kick off time. Many a far side touchline has been quite brilliantly bold and gleaming white with paint having been covered five or six times when Butleigh players have been slower than usual to arrive.

Pre-match hospitality

The pre match mulled wine has promoted a more confident welcome to the visitors. The approach for the last seven years has been to light a

portable gas stove and heat a large aluminium based kettle filled with the cheapest wine available. With the addition of half a bag of caster sugar and some herbs this excellent brew, stirred by a large twig from the neighbouring oak tree, is served to the opposition. Many teams initially view this hospitality with suspicion. This is good news. The effect of cupfuls of simmering mulled wine consumed in the hour before the match is, with the combination of fresh air, thoroughly invigorating and makes light work of the early tackling responsibilities. Butleigh always knows that if the visiting team down the mulled wine with gusto then a more committed match will take place .The effects of drinking the wine before the game are manifold. First it welcomes the opposition, second it helps fill in the hour whilst Butleigh players arrive and, third, it encourages an air of conviviality rather than tension between the two teams in the build up towards kick off.

Actually the six bottles of wine needed to prepare teams before each game became expensive with little change out of twenty pounds. On one occasion the club secretary, Chris Harding, came back from a visit to France with five litre barrels of Vin Ordinaire at two pounds fifty a throw and the club never looked back. The cheapest purchase to date, apart from gifts, was that of two five gallon drums of wine in exchange for two free range ducks which worked out at a pound a gallon. Experiments with mulled cider in the early season games of 2002 were abandoned after attracting a swarm of wasps one of which stung Butleigh tight head prop, Paul Lockyer, on his upper lip making him seem ever more hideously disfigured than he already was. A trial in which we added festive sloe gin to the wine one year was also abandoned after it sent the team into a soporific trance against Wyvern away resulting in Butleigh being five tries down by half time.

Overall the wine appears to be a great success. It accompanies Butleigh on every match home and away, although in a recent flood-lit match against Taunton both the stove and the wine were ordered out of their brand new clubhouse and grandstand complex for fear of setting off the fire alarms. The pre match mulled wine supplies reached undreamed of heights when leading wine distributors Allied Domecque contacted Butleigh looking for a fixture. On 18th March 2004 a home game was arranged and a report was published in the local press.

Butleigh Amateurs 32
Allied Domecque 19

Arriving early Sunday morning there was the hideous discovery at Butleigh's Home ground that some thieving swine had removed the propane gas cylinder and the regulator that was pivotal to heating the former chicken dip tank for the after match bath. Within an hour a new bottle of propane borrowed unknowingly from the village hair dressing salon (later, a little lighter, carefully replaced) plus a gas regulator donated from local farmer, Dave Fry, allowed the water heating system to be exploded into life just as, quite horrifically, the first carload of players arrived from Allied Domecque RFC. Not only were Domecque an hour early but car after car of expensive representative and personalised vehicles, worthy of Earls Court Motor Show, kept arriving.

The Butleigh club captain was keenly aware that many Butleigh players were still in their beds and he commenced, somewhat dejectedly, in a howling gale-swept rainstorm to mark out the pitch. Thirty minutes later prospects improved with the arrival of Allied Domecque's organiser and referee for the day, Graham Turner. Despite having his brightly coloured umbrella turned inside out and just before a particularly effective gust shredded the material off the buckled wires, he presented Butleigh with twenty four bottles of thirteen percent vintage red wine for the pre match mulled wine. Twelve bottles later and the day could not have been more convivial. Butleigh, meanwhile, now boasted nineteen players, and Fatty Edwards had persuaded referee Turner to share pitch duties with each official in charge of one half of the pitch.

The game itself was nicely poised at half time with Allied Domecque leading by twelve points to ten. Mal Hoskins and Will Askam had each scored tries for Butleigh.

An easterly gale lashed down the pitch and much of the game had taken place in Butleigh's half refereed by Mr Turner while Fatty Edwards, the other referee, had looked on, toes touching the half way line. Despite a request by Turner that they should continue to referee in their selected halves, and with the wind continuing unabated, Fatty Edwards oversaw the majority of the play in the second half until an unseemly spat occurred. This was directly due to Edwards awarding a series of unending scrums during a twelve minute period of play when there had been poor handling by both sides. Upon yet another scrum, and just inside Domecque's twenty-two metre line, referee Turner arrived alongside Fatty Edwards.

'You shouldn't allow Butleigh to push before the ball comes in,' he instructed. Edwards indignant at this assistance replied,

'That's only happened once in a sequence of inept play and,' he growled back, 'I've already advised Butleigh not to do so again.'

No more than a minute later the visiting referee was once more at Edwards shoulder – this time only five metres from the try line.

'Didn't you see that knock on?' he shouted, barely audible above the wind. 'What sort of a referee are you?'

Fatty Edwards thoroughly disgruntled with the implications behind this remark drew himself up on his toes.

'Yes, I saw the knock on, but it followed advantage from an accidental offside anyway. What are you doing in my half of the pitch? You've no right to be here, clear off into your own half – and another thing …'

In an age when participants are encouraged towards more civilised conduct between officials and players this magnificent outbreak of verbal hostility between the two referees indicated that under duress human nature often fails to match the calmer waters of considered conduct.

Sometimes players are unavoidably detained. Despite countless calls and promises of, 'if it's Millfield Junior School staff away I'll be there, it's the best game of the season', you can never be sure how the Saturday evening's revelries will leave Butleigh's squad the following morning.

Edgarley Barbarians 19
Butleigh Amateurs 24
The game was played on one of the numerous Millfield Junior School grounds at Edgarley near Glastonbury. Not only is the pitch beautifully marked out but, as it's a Sunday, the boarders are encouraged to watch their teachers play rugby. It's a typically generous gesture to allow the staff to be seen at play not just teaching and controlling discipline. The pristine new school pitch rewarded a significant school following, and the players involved, with the most exhilarating of games.

Edgarley Barbarian captain and organiser, Simon Fuller, had brought together a distinguished staff side which included headmaster Simon Cummings who refereed the first half before taking up playing duties as full back in the second. Dan Close, head of year eight, Paul Denning, a Royal Marine's captain, Adam Duke, an eight hundred metre athlete thinly disguised as a science teacher, Austin Sheppard, ex England and British Lions, Chris Kippax, language teacher, ex Waterloo RFC, Sam Goulby, ex Bristol – the impressive list stretched on.Not only did Edgarley sport a full squad of players but they had replacements to spare, all the result of captain and history teacher, Simon Fuller's months of expert planning.

The significance of this was more than weighing on the Butleigh captain's mind as he cycled off to Glastonbury in search of more Butleigh recruits following a helpful but unsettling phone call from tight head prop Paul Lockyer a few minutes earlier. The call related directly to a significant number of players, the irrepressible youth element of Butleigh, and where they had spent the night before.

It was one thing to go, as they usually did, to Envy night club in nearby Street. The club closed at 1am and, despite the inevitable misunderstandings and the usual fracas involved, most players were at home, or at least someone's home, by 2am. But today this was not the case as revealed by Paul Lockyer's harrowing news.

'London, they're all still in London. They went up after Saturdays' match to this club in Streatham – there's been a bit of a problem. They'll get back as soon as they can. They caught a taxi and they don't know where they are.'

Lockyer went on to explain. Leaving the Streatham night club at three in the morning there had been a hell of a wait for taxis. Well they were in this queue for ages when suddenly a car appeared from nowhere, mounted the pavement wound down the window and shouted, 'Taxi anyone?' Not wishing to overlook the sudden opportunity the lads piled into the car and shouted the name of the bed and breakfast they were booked into. With a squeal of tyres, and a hyper-ventilating turbo cutting in, the car roared off. Anticipation that this was to be a different sort of taxi ride rallied around the fact that the taxi driver seemed not only extremely young but, more worryingly, could barely see over the steering wheel. Radio communications to base were handicapped by the limitations afforded by two leads dangling from an empty dashboard. Initial concerns by the now wide-eyed passengers that the car was not necessarily in the hands of its rightful owner were finally confirmed as the would-be taxi hurtled on through a selection of red traffic lights culminating in unexpected celebrity status as a small battalion of speed cameras flashed into life.

The Butleigh captain's worst fears were confirmed when he eventually spoke to a clearly shocked Hamblin over the phone. 'He didn't have a clue where he was taking us – we hurriedly rounded up some money and thrust twenty quid into his face to stop and drop us off – anywhere, just stop. We fell out of the taxi amazed there hadn't been an accident but we were lost, completely lost, it took us hours to get back – in fact it is midday and we're still in the city.'

The eventual outcome was, with two bottles of port waiting in the changing room, players and friends swapping sides to make up full fifteens and a game that was difficult to better all year.

Seale Hayne Agricultural College 16
Butleigh RFC 0

On the 24th October 1982 the Frank Barber luxury coach clanked noisily away outside the Rose and Portcullis, ready to set off on the day trip to Devon. Inside the pub, the Butleigh squad still awaited some members of the team. 'It's no good', said Berkeley, 'if we don't leave now, there won't be time to have a drink and a sing song and drive back. It's two hours to Seale Hayne.' With that a regular calls in.

'Short of numbers, lads? I've just seen John Abbott playing golf up at Kingweston.'

That was the catalyst. The bar cleared and everyone jumped into the coach, which was directed to the golf course, and arriving minutes later it pulled alongside the green.

'There he is lads,' shouted Cliff Taylor, 'putting on the 8th.'

John Abbott later recounted, 'I was out for a quiet game of golf with John Wigglesworth and a couple of friends when this coach pulled up in the distance and all the people started streaming off and running towards us. I wondered what the hell had happened. Next thing I know is my clubs have been snatched and two of them frog marched me onto the coach. John Wigglesworth followed because I needed a lift home for lunch. When they told me the match was near Taunton, I thought I'd be home by three. It was the other side of Exeter – we didn't kick off until four o'clock and Wigglesworth followed us all the way. We didn't get back until eight. There was a hell of a row at home. God knows what happened to the rest of them. They could be anywhere.'

Training

Opportunities for training also suffer from the 'where is everyone?' syndrome so has largely been abandoned in any formal sense of the word. It's taken place four times in thirty years peaking twice in 1983 and petering out in 1985. Apart from the odd skirmish with a line-out or two before more demanding matches, that's it since no one is quite sure who or what the teams, apart from turning up late, will be. Some players are bigger, more gifted, and fitter than others. Apart from the captain selecting a front row everyone eventually sorts out a position. Providing everyone is introduced to one another prior to the match, and they have actually played rugby at least once before, this works well.

Some, for instance Keith Langoise, who is an artist and designer by trade, was playing for the first time in 1982. He accompanied Butleigh, playing Chard 4th XV away, in Ian MacNab's double-decker bus. The kick off was delayed whilst the bus was extracted from where it had become wedged under a tree on the approach to Chard's out of town pitch. During the match, which went well for Butleigh because many Chard players were playing away in a Cup match, an up and under kick was skilfully fielded by Langoise who was rurally attired in shirt, shorts and Wellington boots for the contest. Cradling the ball as if a fragile porcelain china vase he then, still staring at the ball, asked what he should do with it.

Amongst the farmers that play, prop forward Andy Nixon has converted a disused muck spreader into a rowing machine with a length of rope running twice around the spindle of the spreader and using concrete breeze blocks lashed to the end as weights. Loose head prop Richard Chaddock simply removes the fore end loader off the front of the tractor at the beginning of the rugby season. He then carries hundredweight sacks, propane cylinders, sheep, cattle, pallets around on his shoulders, finally re-attaching the loader at the end of April in time for silaging. Overall training is, unless attempting a higher than comfortable standard, just an excuse for getting out of the house and enjoying a beer with friends after a shower. Stephen Gillam once wrote a treatise on Fatty Edwards' training programme and believed the scheme to be very close to this outcome.

Once, just once, Butleigh came in possession of a scrummaging machine. It arrived from somewhere, obviously following a conversation over a drink. The white machine was wooden and was positioned just to the left of the clubhouse where it was used for parking bicycles and as a clothes stand while changing. Nobody used it for its true purpose but eventually somebody wanted it. Wells rugby club were looking to enhance their scrummaging and so it was sold, possibly via Wells lock forward Greg Cox, for several stacks of canned beer. Proudly it was collected via horse trailer and moved to Wells Rugby Club. Talking to Greg Cox some weeks later, with Butleigh looking for the rest of the agreed crates of beer, inquiries were made into how the machine was settling in.

'Not brilliantly,' said Cox, 'we lined the forwards up for a practise scrum, drove head down into the machine and there was a splintering crunch ...'

The Butleigh players were particularly disappointed because the beer that remained owing was never received.

7. Touring

Following Butleigh's inconclusive, decidedly wet, international selection rugby trials against the Rifleman's Arms away, a sizable touring party of thirty six tourists formally attired in blazer and club tie enjoyed refreshments at the Rose and Portcullis Inn before catching a bus to Bristol Airport.

Arriving at Malaga, a forty-five minute transfer culminated in the team's arrival at Hotel Andeluz in San Pedro, six hundred yards from the Mediterranean and beaches decked with bars. With two hundred rooms, the Spanish, Moroccan-styled hotel had an open-air swimming pool surrounded by cushion-lined deck chairs. It was also host to a large contingent of genteel, polite and correct French families.

An expansive continental breakfast was available each morning ending at 10am sharp, and the majority of rugby tourists arrived for this delight at about 9.30am. The French families counteracted by arriving earlier each morning until they were out-manoeuvred by an increasing number of players returning from all night party vigils. These players arrived back needing coffee and this included a recreational game, cleverly devised by full back Tim Gelfs, of rolling hard-boiled eggs (shell on) down the marble floors towards elderly French couples edging gingerly towards the breakfast area.

Day two and the rugby tour was nicely under way. The first game against Gibraltar had been cancelled and a relaxing ambience, composed of sun, large mixers, sassy music and scantily attired girls filtered over half-closed, shaded eyes, had settled easily upon the touring party. That evening, tour organiser, Tony Berkeley, and Butleigh farmer, front row hooker Kimberley Gane, meandered towards a poolside table. Gane seemed particularly relaxed. Berkeley had the edge.

'Asleep, Gane? You can't get enough of it.'

'You're in the pool, Berkeley.'

'Thirty seven hours in Spain and you've been asleep for thirty six.'

'I'm warning you, any more and you're in.'

There was a pause as Kim Gane slouched on a chair one eye heavy, a hand hovering, waving lazily over a half-filled glass. A catalyst appears – Andy Nixon,

'If he's giving you grief, Kim, push him in. Do you want some help?'

Berkeley, sensing a realistic threat, stepped evasively to one side leaping one corner of the pool, slipping on flat-soled shoes, losing glasses in the tumble and regaining his feet only to be shoved by Nixon into the depths.

A packet of cigarettes bobbed to the surface before Berkeley, intent on revenge, hauled himself out hanging on to the gently-snoring Gane and hauling him into the pool too. Another pack of cigarettes appeared on the surface before the two antagonists using elbows as anchors, Nixon having fled the scene, wedged themselves on the pool surround. Meanwhile six feet below, in shimmering blue water, the tour organiser's mobile phone, the main means of Butleigh's communication with the outside world, lay deep in a watery coma.

Day three passed without incident.

Day four; open side wing forward, Tim Alchin, is building towards a huge fine for not sharing his Swedish liaison of three nights with anyone else. Also for requesting a rebate on his hotel room as he hasn't slept in it

Surface damage.

yet. Fly half Moose, Jon Bath, and Twiglet White also didn't use their room last night having fallen asleep in a skip in Puerto Banus.

Day five; although there hasn't been any rugby yet, players have suffered increasing amounts of surface damage. Brooking Clark was dropped from an unsafe height onto his shoulder, and literally flew out of the Titanic nightclub after becoming involved in a misunderstanding with the Farinas Club bouncer.

Day six; a game of rugby was played against El Monte from Seville who had travelled three and a half hours by coach to play the Butleigh club. This game was a complete shock to the system and very much saved by the focussed attention of former Royal Marine officer, Andy Quinlan. Early on in the match it became apparent that the co-ordination of his team's minds and bodies were operating on separate parallels. An early plan to pass the ball wide to the usually talented back line of Webb, McNab, Harding, Phillips, Gelfs and Sweeney found Butleigh behind by a converted try. Keeping the ball tight with booming touchline kicks by Trigger McNab, following El Monte penalty concessions brought rewards and Quinlan, Taylor and Alchin charged rampantly up the blindside.

Day seven; the teams were summoned for an 11.30am meet for a 1pm kick off against the host team. 'They must be mad – in this heat – thirty four degrees yesterday! No-one's going to be up for it, many have not even returned to the hotel to get up anyway.'

Increasing surface damage.

Taxis arrived at the hotel at 12.15pm. Heroically a large number dragged themselves into the black hearses downing water, red bull and bananas, forcing shattered bodies and minds once more towards sporting endeavour. Two hours later; following a further tortuous sweat-drenched encounter, Butleigh adjourned to base camp, the Palms Bar, for the end of tour court. A grim-faced chief prosecutor, Fatty Edwards, presented horrific allegations of misdemeanours by individuals during the touring week. Hanging judges,

Gane and Webb, with countenances of thunder looked appalled as name upon name was brought forward.

'Minor' offences, we dare go no further, included the following:-

The splintering collapse of Joseph (The Rock) Steadfast-Smythe's hotel bed, following a night of restlessness with a magnificent twenty stone plus beautician, was cited. Pieces of shorn-off slats were produced as evidence. Twiglet White apparently attempted to steal a motor boat, value three million plus. Ivan Garrett fell asleep in a bar, earning a further fine for his dismal defence of having stayed fully awake in the forty seven others visited. Fines were imposed for incidents such as the one where players drained jugs of wine followed by a giddying spin of twenty times around a broom and a sprint across a beach which was previously well-populated by relaxed holiday makers.

As refreshments continued, five of the miscreants wandered to a wooden tower nearby. Thirty metres high, this served as a vantage point for lifeguards.

Constructed in a criss-cross of wooden posts, the tower rose to three stories with each deck protected by railed fencing. The roof, a triangular five-foot square of overhanging thatch, rose to a precise point like a Chinese hat. The young players clambered to the top level. Meanwhile at the Palms Bar sixteen stone prop forward Richard Chaddock saw further opportunities.

Dressed in casual but smart attire with black shoes, Chaddock leapt to his feet, and ran across the beach, delivering on the way a hefty boot into Steadfast whose snoring had developed into a quavering rattle, before sprinting on to the tower. Swiftly climbing the three floors, Chaddock stepped onto the top banister rail before leaning out under the side of the thatched roof clawing for hand holds on the roof itself. The tower appeared fractionally to move. The crowd around the Palms Bar bubbling with laughter, shouts and happy insults hushed at this potentially dangerous manoeuvre.

Chaddock grappled with the seemingly precariously attached roof, his legs swung clear. Nothing now stood between him and a giddying drop to death. Moments of sinew-stretching tension passed as he wrestled himself up onto the thatch and, to the crowd's intense relief, he achieved the summit. The audience breathed again, relaxed that he would surely now come back down. No, not Chaddock; he madly, completely madly, stood up on this uneven, slanting surface calmly raising his hands in presentation.

Under the fragile thatch alarm was evident. Snodgrass White could see the roof buckling under the footsteps above him. Yet the show was barely underway. Chaddock calmly commenced to remove his clothes, nonchalantly dropping them over the roof's edge on to the beach those thirty metres below. A fascinated horror overcame the spellbound audience as, with Chaddock standing first on one foot and then the other, trousers, socks and shorts fell towards the distant ground below. Stark naked, the paragon of individuality raised his arms once more. Climbing back down Chaddock calmly dressed himself before casually strolling back to the rapturously cheering crowd.

The last night of touring following the kangaroo court is payback time, revenge, and the Royal Marines, Quinlan and Marshfield, exacted night manoeuvres on anyone who had caused them grief. Keys, surreptitiously acquired over the week, were used to enter rooms where complete suites of furniture were removed and piled into other rooms already fully furnished. Fire hoses ten times the size of garden equivalents were fed through windows and turned on with occupants awakened by of gallons of surging water jetting out of flailing, snaking hosepipes, drenching them and the entire contents of their room.

1983 – Seville away

Following the hot, dusty, all partying Ferria festival visit to Seville in 1980, during which the rugby was eventually only successful with the help of our host team Club Amigos, organisers, the Reid Brothers, were determined to set new playing standards. With many of the original side having moved away, new players were drafted in. The team was formidable - Metropolitan Police players, Maurice Wood who played wing forward for the British Police, Keith Edmondson (The Winking Bishop) a 6'6" lock forward, Neil Bullock police fly half, Nick Kent the Roundhay centre, combined with a front row of Tim Catley-Day, Kim Gane, Ashley Maunder and supported by a strong second row of Cliff Taylor and John Marshfield.

One player, Dave Weaver, had been in a match for Chew Valley against Butleigh and had caused Butleigh, especially after Butleigh scored first, considerable grief in the close exchanges. It was the Butleigh captain's policy after matches to chat with the opposition and, in particular, to buy their most effective player a couple of pints. He would then invite them to turn out for Butleigh's next match. Weaver, an easily bought mercenary, agreed to play the following week against Blagdon and accepted an invitation to tour to Spain some months later.

A particularly formidable Butleigh pack travelled to Seville this time round.

The flight was non stop entertainment. Every time an air hostess passed by, hands would shoot up in the air with outstretched fingers giving marks out of ten. The team congregated at the back of the plane where they

Butleigh in Seville 1983.

Butleigh vs Seville, at Kingweston 1984.

commandeered the drinks trolley. Songs were sung and a rugby ball was thrown backwards and forwards across the plane just clearing other passengers' heads. There was a five hour wait at Santiago because our connecting flight had taken off without us. The airline issued free drinks vouchers which the friendly bar steward interpreted as a free bar as long as Butleigh were there. By the time we caught the next flight to Malaga the party was in slight disarray.

The Butleigh captain had already lost one player – wing forward Andy Harvey who had consumed the pilot's personal rations, special milk and hidden the emergency exit key on the way over, had had a row with organiser, Robin Reid, and disappeared catching a flight to somewhere else; never seen him again to this day. Winger Matthew Holbert having manfully, and with some assistance, scaled the steps to the connecting flight was then unwell, taken off, and rushed to hospital by the overzealous Spanish airport doctors. Rupert Reid went with him to look after him. And then, just when Butleigh were on their last warning to behave themselves, Stuart Forsey, sitting quietly but mischievously in his seat, exploded a well shaken champagne bottle with a terrific bang. The cork flew towards the front of the plane. Twenty years later and in the current climate no one could risk these antics.

Arriving, finally, in Seville our hosts were understandably reluctant to offer house hospitality. By the early hours Taylor was only standing upright by clinging onto a car windscreen wiper, Marshfield had passed out in the back of the same vehicle. Everyone had to sort out their own accommodation. Part of the problem was that the recent Falklands war, for which Spain was sympathetic to Argentina, meant the English tourists were given a cold shoulder, with occasional demands of 'Why? Why the war?'

The following day was the low point, Dave Weaver and his mate Gerald Higgins wanted to fly home - everyone felt hung-over - a training session was organised but the Spanish wouldn't lend us a ball to replace the one we had lost, so we trained with a round cornered, cylindrical, breeze block, mauled it for minutes on end up and down a rough sandy pitch with neglected rust red rugby posts – the weather was hot – unbelievably hot – dusty – choking – everyone sweated – everyone drank water – bottles and bottles until the end of the session, then it was a return to normality and San Miguel lagers.

Next day Butleigh was involved in a rugby tournament and also involved in the hardest match of their lives. Davina Pastora – Away. Ten minutes into the game near exhaustion, centre Nick Kent jogged wearily over to the Butleigh forwards.

'Guys, guys,' he gasped. 'I can't keep this level of tackling up; you've got to hold onto it.' Rupert Reid called everyone in. 'Right this is the tactic. It's a forwards ball from now on. You do NOT pass the ball out until you have made the opposition twenty two – on NO account – until I say – do you release the ball.'

So began the most gruelling two halves of rugby imaginable. In the heat and dust, the ball was mauled yard after yard up the pitch – Spanish boots flayed English heads: knees and fists smashed into Spanish bodies, grunts, shouts, blood, spit and more and more mauling until far into the second half, having made the twenty two, the ball was finally spun from Butleigh scrum half Hugh Nicholson Lailey to fly half Neil Bullock who dummied then crashed over for the game's only try. With minutes to go, Nick Kent struck a drop goal – Butleigh won 7-0.

If the first cup match with Taunton cemented the club's team spirit, this game saved the tour and made the rest of the week into the greatest rugby playing ever. The singing, the celebrations, the relief, the belief, the ecstasy of winning seemingly the hardest of matches two thousand miles from home sealed the future – Rugby tours were (for twenty years) only going one way – back to Spain. Butleigh went on to win the competition final against Gibraltar before travelling south west to Puerto St Maria for a first visit and win against CRAP, club rugby al Puerto, a town we were to tour every two years from 1990, alternating with Marbella in 1998 and 2002.

The Tour Court in Puerto 1994
The court began with a few minor cases to warm up the ever appreciative audience, which had now been swelled with family members of the Puerto club who had heard about the tour court and turned up to watch 'the mad Engleesh' do their bit.

'The penultimate case, your honour, concerns two gentlemen who abandoned ship without permission.' Fatty Edwards drew himself up to his full and substantial height and launched himself into a prosecution address that would have convinced any jury. But he needn't have bothered, by now the audience was begging for action. 'This court of your peers,' he boomed, 'having found you guilty, sentence you to the dance of the flaming ****holes.'

'Oh no, not that,' pleaded Moose. He could not escape, toilet paper having been appropriately placed, followed by setting ablaze with a cigarette lighter and the dance commenced. The only method permitted of extinguishing the flames is to leap hop and bounce up and down. Many a fraught participant has ended up in the cloakroom, sitting in a wash basin filled with cold water.

'We now come to the last case, m'lud. We have in our company a person of strange habits - one who likes wearing women's clothing whilst enjoying the vibrational benefit of strange, and surely improper, electrical apparatus. The prosecuting council therefore calls Mr Christopher White to the dock.'

What colour was on Chris White's face immediately disappeared as his countenance took on the colour of his name. 'Not fair,' he stammered. 'I didn't pack my suitcase, it was my girlfriend, she obviously wanted to – to pack something to remind me of her.'

Prosecutor Edwards was having none of it. 'I think, m'lud that the defendant should wear the offending apparel so that the court might appreciate the full nature of his crime.' Chris White once possibly had a fine athletic body, over six feet and well muscled but time had passed on and the strain of too many cervezas was in evidence around his waistline and besides that he wasn't his girl friend's size ten!

Greeted by the sight of Chris White stepping into a lacy teddy designed to show enough to keep the viewer guessing, but in his case managing to reveal more than it hid, members of the court and spectators in the gallery hurriedly covered their vulnerable eyes. A beer thrust into his hand and downed in one finished the punishment.

'Court adjourned, fresh glasses please.'

Another tour had come to a close. The players disappeared out into the night for one final look around Puerto with new found friends. For the 1994 tourists it was a confirmation of all things Butleigh Rugby stood for. Fast open rugby, played with a fierce unswerving commitment to your fellow players, for memorable times and the meeting of old friends and of making new ones, for the joy and strength of true camaraderie, for the joy of rugby.

J. R Farrow 2005

Preparing the pitch

Butleigh RFC vs a London XV, late 1970s

The Chicken Dip Tank

The After Match Bath

The Butleigh Summer Ball

Loughborough University, winners of the Magnificent Sevens 2005

£2400 donated to St John's Ambulance, Street

Away to the Honourable Artillery Company, London

8. Girls, romance and international renown

> *'The fundamental trouble with marriage is that it shakes a man's confidence in himself and so greatly diminishes his general competence and his effectiveness. His habit of mind is that of a commander who has calamitously lost a decisive battle. He never quite trusts himself thereafter.'*
>
> H. L. Mencken, Prejudices: Second Series, 1920.

Love them, hate them, need them, think about them; feed them, financially a turbo charged vacuum cleaner linked to a cash machine. More emotionally demanding than yourself, beguiling but when the right one comes along, fascinating and life enhancing.

Lucy Chaddock is quite magnificent. She's a brunette with shoulder length hair, sparkling eyes, striking good looks and a svelte figure – more inside centre than wing forward. A fearless tackler, and with a brain the size of a planet, she organises the black tie Summer Ball and humbles the opposition in after match celebrations. Lucy not only comes along to the rugby matches but is available in case of injury or Butleigh are short of players or she just plays anyway. In a match against Blake's Bears of Bridgwater, Lucy came on as a replacement and within minutes, in an all encompassing slightly high tackle, she pole axed the opposition's winger who not only seemed rendered unconscious but turned an unusual colour. Against Weston away, following a cup match, Weston's best down-in-one pint drinker was summoned to a contest against Butleigh's finest. Lucy with an empty glass left him spluttering with a quart to go. Against Clifton at home in Butleigh, the Clifton captain was challenged to down a pint in one partially as a distraction to their team's coach being sent home by a Butleigh player pretending to be one of the visitors. It was the captain's 9th, 10th and 11th pint. Lucy won 2 – 1. Half an hour later he was wandering the local lanes looking for a coach that was no longer there.

Clare Daniels who captained the local Tor women's rugby proved a girl above thousands by becoming a referee and rocketing in a precocious few years up the refereeing scale - now officially at level 5. Such is Clare's professionalism that in a recent cup match involving Butleigh and Castle Cary she sin binned three Butleigh players, including Nixon. He exacted revenge by borrowing her cards when she played scrum half for Butleigh, six months later sin binning her in the second half for 'persistent flouting the laws of rugby'.

Clare Daniels, Lockyer, Wright and Stead.

The girls have a noticeable the effect on the regular Butleigh players. One night stands or short term relationships hardly interrupt a player's overall commitment, however serious relationships often see a player disappear from the rugby scene for up to 18 months. Marriage was often a disaster – some were never seen again – not even for a social beer, as if lost by alien abduction. Many girls were terrific news for the club always enjoying the company and humour of everyone. Some enjoyed the company of farmers particularly relishing close activity within the cabs of high revving tractors as they ploughed up and down the rutted fields of local farmland, hands on the throttle levers, knowing just when to increase the power output.

The girls always had their favourites and wing forward Andy Foot was a popular request. 'The great thing about Footy,' commented a feisty girl friend 'is that he is such a great handyman.'

Apparently, having wrecked and destroyed the bed one night he dived under the bed with hammer, screws and supporting wooden struts to repair it before resuming his affections. Trigger MacNab usually brings his girlfriend along to the match. Once, just once, Trigger was appointed captain of Butleigh in a home match against Blakes Bears from Bridgwater. At half time Butleigh were trailing 12-10. If ever a captain's half time talk was needed it was this day. New tactics, a different attack plan was urgently required. Trigger however surprised everyone by jogging off the field and climbing into his car alongside his new girlfriend and slamming the door shut. Over the five minute break not only did the car door stay shut but the windows began misting up and the car began rocking. Trigger's neglectful captaincy resulted in not only no half time talk but playing the first ten minutes of the second half without him on the pitch. Finally the door opened and Trigger returned nonchalantly to the pitch to continue in the game.

Butleigh has also been a sanctuary for those down on their luck, for instance a player married for a number of years suddenly goes through a

period of domestic hell at home and there he is back at the ground drinking a cup of mulled wine seeking favourable understanding company looking for his place back in the team.

Relationship psychoanalyst Andy Nixon reflected on marriage one Sunday following an abandoned match. Now involved with the second brew of pre-match fortified wine, Nixon declared that, when arriving at South Barrow from his Hampshire farm some five years before, 'Somerset was a county full of victims of divorce. The farmers,' he said, 'previously sports mad enthusiasts involved in feasts on barons of beef and barrels of cider have been turned into second time round, timorous, domesticated cash machines.'

'In the golden era,' continued Nixon, 'you would see gatherings of those clear eyed farmers in rude health, pockets full of notes to buy drinks over the bar and blow wild life out of the skies both combined with weekly social outings to their local market. Now, they look haggard and forlorn with a constant handing out of money to women, like a desperate sparrow gathering worms for nagging nestlings.'

Nixon illustrated his observations with an appalling tale of neglect about Brusher, one eventually with a happy ending. Brusher, beer barrel buster and Dorchester and Dorset county lock forward was a favoured guest in Fatty Edward's Twickenham hospitality tent. A 6'5" socialite farmer, he would barely miss any sporting occasion. Shooting, hunting, Point-to-Point, skittles, any event where two or more gathered with fun in mind, and Brusher would be in the thick of it. One day, however, it all tragically ended when his wife left. Between her and the Divorce Court Judge, he was sentenced to hard labour in his own milking parlour, milking his own cows. Brusher went spiralling down hill, no more outings, only rare sightings of the man, wasting away, a forlorn figure trudging bewildered around supermarket aisles. After several years of non-attendance, Brusher reappeared at Twickenham for a recent England v South Africa match, back to his old self, several stone heavier, in the centre of the festivities, having been rescued by a new partner, the daughter of one of Dorset's Beef Barons. 'This,' concluded Nixon 'is why men like Fatty Edwards are dinosaurs of a species. Heritage orders must be placed on them.'

Acts of great courage have accompanied Butleigh players; not least when prop forward Paul Riley who once, on a return trip from the Bath's Pulteney Arms, upon spying a large double decked table full of attractive pot plants requested the van to pull over. He wished to take some flowers home to his girl friend. Leaping out of the van, ignoring the nearby honesty box, Riley to everyone's astonishment picked up the whole display and staggering across to the van heaved the trestle and sixty plants with one dramatic swing into the back. The van with earth and stones everywhere became an instant flower bed, one that a herd of beasts had trampled through. Over the following miles flower pots were gradually assembled on the dashboard of the van, giving an attractive horticultured appearance to oncoming traffic.

Riley, believing he possessed a gift of instant charm whilst on rugby tour in Puerto was queuing in a particularly elegant Spanish Bank to cash in travellers cheques. Moving to the bank's exchange till and spying a particularly attractive cashier he unzipped the front of his trousers and producing a significant part of his anatomy, presented it at the window asking whether she would be able to change it for him.

Tight head prop Paul Lockyer, in his younger day was enjoying the post marriage celebrations of England International Philippa's wedding in a large marquee. Wearing his outfit for all occasions, a black zipped leather jacket, 5'8" Lockyer was minding his own business, consuming pints of Somerset cider when he was plucked from party obscurity by a tall international female player, and escorted to the dance floor. Gripping the lapels of his jacket, she lifted him with ease onto his tip toes for a slow dance and matters moved apace when she extended the liaison by removing Lockyer from the floor out through a far exit of the marquee and onto the nearby cricket pitch.

Preparing the cricket square for a match the following day the head grounds-man was appalled at the damage accrued at one end of the cricket square.

'There were scuff marks and rakings as if a pair of wild animals had ripped into the turf, God only knows what caused the damage,' he said.

Butleigh's International Player

Butleigh has one - she is Philippa Atkinson. Five feet ten, blonde bombshell, a turbo charged Lara Croft, fit, fast and athletic. Her commitment improves every person, team, and situation that she's involved with. The Butleigh winger introduces herself to her friends with a flying tackle. One Saturday, Pip played in an England vs. Scotland women's international and, next day, spotted an old acquaintance, Andy Wolstenholme, coach to Blackheath Club and the England team.

'I saw Andy in the distance with some guy, hadn't seen him for years,' she explained. 'Ran along flat out and did a complete tackle on him, round the ankles, floored him!'

'Who the heck's that?' shouted Andy's friend.

'Meet Pip,' gasped a winded Wolstenholme.

'Pleased to meet you,' said former England wing forward Mickey Skinner extending a hand to pull Pip up off the ground. 'Is this your normal style of greeting friends?'

Pip (3rd left, front row) with Butleigh RFC in 1984.

Following the Scottish Classics Rugby Tournament, Pip instigated bar diving. You leap high into the air off the bar to be caught by two lines of players, arms linked. They then bounce you up and down, trampoline style, while you try to fire a champagne cork out of your mouth into a distant ashtray. Later that same evening, feeling a little peckish, Pip spotted another friend, Tosh Askew, under 19 coach, in a busy, genteel restaurant and tackled him full on. Later that evening she was spotted on the shoulders of a six foot five, All Hallows Boy, with a Pooh Bear thong on her head, singing 'Mustang Sally'.

Following the Butleigh Magnificent Sevens, one year, Pip invited three Internationals Lisa Burgess, Georgia Stevens and Suzie Appleby to play in an invitation Clifton vs. Taunton women's rugby match as a curtain raiser to the final. There was a hitch right at the end of the day. Pip says,

'We had been watching my cousin Steve Gillam's Blues Band playing at the Rose and Portcullis. Having left, we later realised that a friend had left her coat and keys in the pub. We had banged on windows and doors there was but no response. Then Colonel Ian Saunders appeared and, on hearing the story, he suggested going round to the front where a hatch sized window could be prized open. Standing on Saunders's shoulders I squeezed half way through before becoming stuck on zips and dropping back onto the ground outside.'

At this point the Colonel said, 'I'm going in,' and with great gallantry, he forced his torso up, in and halfway through the window, dangling his legs with Pip holding on. Unfortunately he passed the fulcrum of balance. 'Release me slowly,' he gasped heaving once more. With that he disappeared with a deafening crash, tumbled head first on one of the lounge table tops and lay there, unmoving.

'Christ, he's broken his neck,' shouted Pip and wriggled furiously through the same window, jeans tearing on the hook, before she too fell through with a thumping crunch, her fall softened by landing directly on top of the Colonel's slumped figure. This, against the odds, brought him round. Suddenly a mighty din erupted as all the pubs alarm sensors were triggered but, even worse, the sound of furious barking accompanied creaking floorboards above. The landlords were finally responding to the break in. With that a door was flung open and the pub's Alsatian lunged across the carpet towards them. What appeared to be a shot gun flickered in the red strobe effect of the security alarms.

'Get out of our pub. Get out, get out,' shouted the landlord. 'The police are coming, get out.'

Pip Kennedy's career -

1981-1983 - watch Cousin Robert Laver and boyfriend playing for Butleigh.
1984 – Playing first games for Butleigh RFC and competing in the modern pentathlon at Loughborough University. She carries on her story,

'I was training one Sunday, preparing for national triathlon championships. Mary Cheetham saw me and asked if I fancied a game of rugby as I looked 'quite quick'. That afternoon my debut appearance for Loughborough University women's rugby team was against Edmonton,

Pip (3rd left, back row) with the England team in 1992.

Canada, who were touring the UK. I played on the wing and remembered all the skills I picked up with Butleigh. I was hooked! I was then fortunate enough to persuade Jim Greenwood – ex British Lions/Scotland – to coach Loughborough 1st XV women's rugby team. This meant I was then instructed by one of the most respected rugby coaches in the world. He went on to coach our regional side, 'Midlands'. In 1986 I was selected to represent Great Britain, the first ever international women's rugby match to be played in the UK, GB vs. France at Richmond where we lost to the French.

'The GB side was made up of some influential and later superstar women rugby players – Lisa (Big Bird) Burgess most capped Welsh woman rugby player – Amanda Bennett – Welsh coach, and now backs coach to England woman's XV, and Karen Almond – captain of England women's XV who won the World Cup. In 1986 the team was 'Great Britain' because there were not enough players to create an England team. However, women's rugby grew so quickly that in April 1987 the first England vs. Wales match at Pontypool Park saw England win a game in which I scored a hat trick of tries. I then went to France to play GB vs. France before setting off to Australia for a change of scenery. Within weeks of arriving I was playing National League women's and mixed touch rugby in Sydney. Returning to the UK in 1989 – I played rugby for Newport and represented Welsh Counties.

'I moved over the bridge to coach/play for Clifton WRFC taking them from 2nd to 1st division and then coached the Clifton 7's team for National 7's Championship. We overcame Saracens in the semi final and beat Wasps in the final. I regard this as my biggest achievement – coaching and playing for a second division side to beat the best of the 'big guns'. In the National 7s, Clifton became the first south west team to win the title. Coming off the pitch – hand on shoulder from England manager Genevieve Shaw, 'Would you like to play for England in an international match at the Caldy 7s?'

'We played Scotland and the England coach asked whether I would play for England once more. I thought I'd give it a go and started training with the England squad in 1996. I also coached England's 7s team to play in the inaugural Hong Kong women's 7s competition. 1997 was an amazing year. After England won the Women's Five Nations Championship, I flew out to Hong Kong to become 1st coach/player of the England women's team and we made the semi finals vs. USA - then off to the European championships before, six weeks later, touring New Zealand. Following a major injury, picked up in training, it was a big push to prepare for 1998 World Cup in Holland, however I was selected for the squad. I announced my retirement from international rugby after the semi final in which we lost to The Black Ferns.'

Since retiring from International rugby, Pip teaches and coaches at Wells Cathedral School - the first woman to coach an independent school 1st XV. Her husband, Pete, says, 'Pip was one of the few to set the standard for modern day fitness in women's rugby. She is undoubtedly a very special girl – a Butleigh girl.'

England Players Martin Corry - and Phillipa.

9. The Magnificent Sevens and Fund-raising

The Chairman – Colin Gravatt

Arriving from New Zealand, Colin Gravatt began work for BOCM Animal Feeds specialising in poultry feeds. The Butleigh club captain who reared turkeys and ducks had a firm policy concerning the feeding of his flocks. It didn't matter what the company was or how excellent their food product was the main criteria for purchasing livestock pellets was that the representative must play rugby for Butleigh. Notable feed reps involved over the years would have included prop forward Nigel Weaver, hooker Phil Brady and prop, wing forward Colin Gravatt.

When Gravatt arrived in this locality he joined top Dorset and Wilts rugby side Devizes and, within a year, became their player coach. Not only did Gravatt therefore excel as a Kiwi rugby player but within months, as fixtures between Butleigh and Devizes blossomed, other significant players such as Steve Pearce, Chris Jones and Tim Alchin became regulars for Butleigh. These, and others, were seriously useful individuals. Moose and Alchin played for their county and many of the others were first teamers (Southern Counties level). Gravatt, based in Devizes quite brilliantly fell for and married a Butleigh girl, Cindy Stock, and moved to Castle Cary. Soon, he was not only helping organise teams and fundraising events but he

became a supporter of the Magnificent Sevens. He raised its profile from five to six teams under inspirational founder Stephen Gillam to a twelve and then sixteen team bonanza with the tournaments played on August Bank Holiday Sunday. Tim and Clare Gelfs, with Lucy Chaddock and Andy Foot, organise a two hundred seat black tie Summer Ball. The Magnificent Sevens take place two days later. The weekend is the club's biggest event of the year.

Gravatt is also one of life's rarities – not only does he do what he says he is going to do but if he allocates or someone volunteers to do a job within the club you just know that Gravatt is going to phone, shortly to find out how they are progressing. If you haven't started he'll phone back a few days later to see if you now have and if you still haven't fulfilled your obligation he'll suggest that if there's a problem he will come round and help you work it out. He's tenacious, relentless, persistent, and honest and always sees projects through. This makes him an excellent chairman. Someone that Butleigh in the early years would have had difficulty in coping with.

Take the example of Butleigh's triumphant reconnection twenty two years after being cut off by the equivalent of Wessex Water in 1981 due to the finicky detail of not having paid a water bill for three years. A front loader was used to clear out Stephen Gillam's shed and earth was excavated. Nixon and Gravatt then laid a six foot concrete base on top of hard core chippings. This was monumental progress for a clubhouse that had gently fallen into disrepair over three decades.

A trench was dug towards the village's mains pipe from the proposed after match washroom bath area and the water board contacted. Then for a huge fee of £320 the club was connected to the mains via a water meter sunk into the ground. Covered with earth it's now virtually untraceable. Three months after accomplishing the Herculean task a water board inspection was insisted upon involving an official visiting Butleigh's new washroom to declare it valid and legal. Chairman Gravatt courageously volunteered to oversee the inspection so that at eight o'clock on Monday morning, February 17th, 2003, the inspector of installations for Wessex Water board stood, shivering, staring at Butleigh rugby club's luxurious controversial washing down facilities on Kingweston village green. Peering over the lip of the four hundred gallon cattle trough he winced at the muddy, ice covered sediments lying in the bottom.

'How many people used this facility yesterday?' he quizzed.

'Thirty plus,' replied Gravatt.

'And you fill this full of cold water, direct from the mains?'

Gravatt paused for a moment, struggling to gauge whether the mention of the 625 horse powered tractor driven dynamometer that heats the water might be too much information for the occasion.

'Right to the top,' he replied.

The inspector closed his eyes, shuddering at the prospect. After a moment's composure he peered into the gloom towards the back of the cobweb laced shed. 'A new tap,' he observed, 'but where is the pipe leading to and from it?'

'There isn't one,' said Gravatt, 'it's to stop any children from meddling with the supply when we're not around.'

The inspector stared at a new brass tap nailed to a distant wooden stanchion.

'So what's that for?'

Gravatt, keenly aware that the inspector was coming to the most delicate part of the proceedings, lowered his voice replying with focussed concern.

'To comply with water board regulations we were instructed to install a tap with a non-return valve which, I think you'll agree, we have achieved. Which also isn't connected to a pipe,' he grimly observed. The Wessex water board representative pursed his lips and in a vain attempt to assert some authority within the visit declared, 'That tap however,' pointing at the isolated item, 'legally needs to be eighteen inches above the water line of the bath.'

'In which case,' said Gravatt, 'we'll move it.'

'And,' continued the inspector, 'if, God forbid, your club attempts to install any system of hot water heating facilities within these,' he paused, 'unusual premises then you must inform the water board immediately.'

'Meanwhile,' he went on, 'I'll post my findings to you once I've discussed this situation with my superiors. Good day to you.'

Drawing his jacket ever tighter, the official, clipboard clenched under one arm, marched back to the warmth of his car. Colin Gravatt drew in a long deep breath. Somewhere within the water board's inspection Butleigh had possibly secured a victory over officialdom. He just hoped upon hope that something such as the Health and Safety department would never become involved.

Gravatt is a quite magnificent, effective chairman, a terrific communicator and full of enthusiasm for new ventures whilst keeping an eye on the basic structure of the club. Colin, along with Pip Kennedy and Andy Foot, has been instrumental in founding Butleigh's Tag rugby for children where up to seventy children run out on Tuesday evenings and now participate in Tag rugby tournaments.

He is a tremendous promoter of fund raising activities.

The Magnificent Sevens

'The trouble with Butleigh,' said Referee Bob McCumpsky, sitting in Tor Leisure bar in Glastonbury in 1992, 'is, that they don't give anything back to rugby, it's all one way.'

Butleigh full back and blues rock singer, Stephen Gillam, pondered the statement, felt Butleigh did a lot for the game but, nevertheless, a chord was struck. The following year, with assistance from hooker Mark Wilkinson, the first Butleigh 7's started with six teams on August Bank Holiday Sunday. The competition was won by Perry's Perverts, a team from Tor Rugby Club. A phone call at midday to Colonel Ian Saunders as to where the Wells rugby side were, revealed that he thought the competition was on the Monday. However, rallying himself, he arrived at the pitch within the hour, with stocks of Tennents lager. Setting up camp at one end of the field, he drew a side together with the offer of free beer.

A week later Gillam and Wilkinson met, as they did every day, at the Rose and Portcullis, and counted out the takings from the burger stall, a raffle and entry fees of twenty pounds a team. Some hours later with the bolts on the pub being eased across, the two charity fund raisers walked, still feeling some slight trepidation of school authority, into Butleigh Primary School where they knocked on the head mistress's door. When it opened

they thrust £350 cash into her surprised hands.

The Magnificent Sevens in the early days. Former President Bill Roberts in the Car.

'This is for the school from Butleigh Rugby Club, please put it towards something useful for the children.'

The Seven-a-Side Rugby tournament has become a huge part of Butleigh's calendar and it is a wonderful fundraiser. It had modest beginnings in the 'Tented Village' days set around an ancient marquee which was made up of green khaki canvas and was almost impossible to raise when damp. It was exceedingly frail, with numerous rips and tears. Six splintered posts fitted into three sockets and, when latched together, held up the tent. Pulling the tent up required a car with a tow hitch having a rope attached to it via the top of the tent which was still lying on the ground. The car was then driven steadily away whilst assistants thrust their feet into the base of the three uprights. Crunching, cracking and shredding noises would accompany the raising of the canvas which would be steadied, once up,

while iron bars and single eyed hooks were driven into the ground.

Accompanying the tent was free entertainment for children with the hire of a bouncy castle and a generator from a farm in Radstock. Whilst very popular, the castle, due to no one checking the fuel in the generator or tripping over extension cables, would deflate several times during the afternoon with children trapped inside.

Over the years the competition developed, teams crept up to eight and more funds were raised. A donation was always made to a youth organisation within Butleigh.

Dai, Sophie and Pam Roberts.

The revenues grew and tens of thousands of pounds were raised. The NSPCC, Guide Dogs for the Blind, a Defibrillator for St John's Ambulance, Horses for the Disabled and St Margaret's Hospice in Yeovil all benefited. The main catalyst for widening the event even further was the enthusiastic and effective impact of New Zealander Colin Gravatt.

With a committee of friends, he developed the competition to the sixteen team tournament it is today. Sixteen teams and only one pitch take some vision to organise. In the early rounds, two matches are ongoing, played across the pitch. Then the whole ground is opened up for the semi finals and final so it is, amazingly, possible. Undoubtedly the greatest asset has been the introduction of a broadcast system from Glastonbury FM's mobile studio to give information about when each team is playing next, and which referee is needed, whilst prior games are being played. The first year this was attempted an amplifier from Steve Gillam's Blues Band, Idle Frets, was borrowed. Whilst this was on a straw bale it worked brilliantly for an hour. Then, due to variable output from a small petrol generator, it started smoking and caught fire.

Recent years have also linked the Butleigh Ball, staged in a vast, six sectioned marquee which is held over for the Sevens on Sunday. The dinner entertains about 200 guests and awards are presented for the previous year's endeavours. In the early days the dinner was held at the Wessex Hotel in Street and in 1983, following a tremendously successful tour to Seville, a large gathering assembled in extremely hot weather. There was no air conditioning, the guests were in formal outfits and the after dinner entertainment was 'Jeff the Breath', an enthusiastic fire eater. Gathering everyone's attention, Jeff blew a huge blast of impressive orange flame that rose up and travelled over the heads of the already wilting guests.

James Phillips receives the trophy from Phil Gristock.

There is a prestigious trophy for the winner of the 7s tournament, the battered saucepan. The history of this unique piece of 'silverware' dates to 1987 when percussion player, Guy Pursey, on tour with Butleigh in Seville was looking for a bongo drum to accompany the Gillam, Berkeley, Laver

trio. Passing a skip, he instantly recognised the musical potential of this handy saucepan. Mark Wilkinson, having tripped over a loose piece of paving slab, realised this would make the base and with a screw edged top, thrust through a drilled hole in the saucepan, so the trophy was created. For a number of years the battered saucepan stood on the trophy shelf littered with bottles and various mementos lifted from away days. It appeared once at the Butleigh presentation dinner and a frozen pigs head, which had been won against the H.A.C. in London, sat gently defrosting over the evening giving the trophy a somewhat personal fragrance that year.

Teams each year have included representatives from Richmond, Loughborough, Bridgwater, Yorkshire, Swanage and Wareham, vying

with local sides of Wincanton, Somerton, Wells and Tor. There are also the legends of local characters who make up their own teams of The Rifleman's Deviants, HLCT (Hands Like Cow's Tits) and the Mighty Ducks. The Ducks, led by Steadfast Smythe, bring their own swimming pool in which they not only sensibly store all their cans of Extra Strong lager and cider but wallow in between games. The HLCT bring their own mascot a pantomime cow which, traditionally, when the effects of the day set in takes a place in the three quarter line. The Deviants are fuelled on cider making them, depending on the time of the day, one of the more unpredictable sides to play against. They can be quite brilliant.

However it was the Welsh side, Hafodrynys, that caught the eye over a three year visit before a dramatic pitch invasion by their supporters brought a mutually colourful acquaintance to a close. Organised by the landlord of the Travellers Rest, Hafodrynys players and supporters first appeared in a large coach in 1999. Despite losing their two pool matches due to a side withdrawing and despite having not scored a try they reached the final of the Plate competition. The following year this village team reappeared, picnic baskets, teenagers in lust, mothers, dads, with a stronger team and made the semi finals of the main competition being ousted by James Phillip's crack side of North Wootton. On the following, and what was to be the last, visit an even finer squad was assembled. The presence of a Welsh under 21 International was stimulating. Confidence was high, noise was louder, gas horns blaring out, with ringing cheers for every try scored, every match won. Even better, Hafodrynys made the final. With touchlines packed, competition organiser, Stephen Gillam, was fraught, indeed he was beside himself.

'The cups not going back with them!' he said. 'We'll never see it again.'
The match against opposition finalists North Wootton, ten minutes each

way, kicked off and Wootton went two tries up. The Wootton winger cupped his hand to his ear goading the Welsh supporters as he raced in for another try. Hafodrynys, with a sense of injustice, ripped back with a score then another before half time. Wootton, the previous year's winners were just edging out the feisty, more muscular Welsh by a score into the last five minutes. Every time Wootton scored, back roared the Welsh until, with two minutes to go, controversy erupted.

The problem was partly that the Welsh and English supporters had encroached on the nearside trackline and linesman Bob McCumpsky had spent much of the game waving, guiding and ordering spectators off the pitch. With time running out, Hafodrynys had with dramatic play not only forced themselves into a promising position just inside Wootton's 22 metre line but, crucially, been awarded a penalty. In achieving this potential match winning area the Welsh outside centre had delivered a healthy punch to his opposite number. McCumsky, in a rare moment of not having his back to the game had noticed this and promptly raised his flag to attract the attention of future international referee Miss Clare Daniels. Having awarded the penalty to the Welsh side Miss Daniels had a certain amount of niggling apprehensions as she consulted the linesman regarding his intervention. 'Foul play within a late tackle,' confirmed Bob, 'reverse the penalty.' The subsequent pitch invasion, where the entire Welsh village wished to express their concern over the penalty reversal, would have possibly been one of Miss Daniels' defining moments as to whether to continue her meteoric refereeing career or retire gracefully. Wootton hung on to win the tournament. Hafodrynys returned home, aggrieved, via The Traveller's Rest and, after three noisy, controversial years, they have decided to rest matters. We hope that one day they will return.

Clare is refereeing in the woman's World Cup in Canada this autumn.

More fund-raising activities

Chris Harding says, 'The City Sevens is a phenomenon well worth attending. It is a festival of rugby for the business houses of the City of London. It is also another important charity event in the rugby world raising thousands every year for S.P.A.R.K.S. the children's charity. There you will see the young bloods from the world of finance battling it out on the fields of the Richmond Athletic Ground.

'The teams to be encountered are basically made up from the business house employees but ringers are not unknown. Such wonderful names appear in the programme; Lloyds of London, the Stock Exchange, Deutch Bank and Allan and Overy, the solicitors. It is more a day for festive corporate hospitality than anything else. Marquees abound, barbeque smoke gets in your eyes and the prettiest girls in London are drawn to the tournament to be fought out by healthy and wealthy young males. It is in many ways the modern equivalent to the medieval tournament when knights in armour jousted for the favour of their lady. And what has this got to do with Butleigh? As ever, it is a long story.

'At the time that I made my 'epic' speech to the RFU my comments fell on the ears of Keith Sheppard, secretary to the London Stock Exchange RFC and master mind of the City Sevens. Apparently the idea of an Amateur club was music to Keith's ears. Offering support to the amateur cause, with one of the twenty five votes, he later approached Butleigh requesting an inspection visit to Somerset. All was arranged. Keith was invited for the weekend. He inspected the field, watched a match and was fed and watered in the Rose and Portcullis. He loved the anachronism that was Butleigh. The inspection complete, by way of reciprocal hospitality, he offered Butleigh a place in the City Sevens. Butleigh was to be the second invitation side that year; the other was the Paris Borse, the French Stock Exchange.

'The great day arrived. As usual the team selection was somewhat haphazard and at the appointed meeting time at the Rose and Portcullis there was a scarcity of playing talent. Fortunately the nocturnal abodes of the guilty absentees were known and phone calls summoned the errant lovers to their duties for the club. The team reached London. The captain, Ashley, followed on behind in his butcher's van. The President, Bill Roberts, followed on too in his celebrated Butleigh 2CV Citroen. On reaching the gate, Ashley, dressed in his white butcher's coat and white hat, leant out of the window shouting to the gateman, 'Catering'. Sure enough he was admitted without question and he immediately drove to the VIP car park. Straw bales and cider barrels were unloaded and the slim evidence of catering, bread and cheese, was unloaded. The multi coloured 2CV followed and the Butleigh camp was set up; the party began.

'At the end of the day, it was realised that no trophy had been secured. At six o'clock precisely Lance Farrell solemnly approached the flagstaff. He lowered the City Sevens flag, with REUTERS, the sponsors, all over it, secured the halyards, folded the flag neatly and returned with the full dignity of his position to the Butleigh base. There he secreted the flag into a space in the van. A trophy indeed; it is now on display at the Rose and Portcullis.'

S.P.A.R.K.S. the children's charity 2005.

Butleigh's fundraisers

*The Butleigh
Ball*

*Butleigh RFC
in the mid
1980s.*

Tor President's XV	14
Butleigh Amateur President's XV	17

The match, a curtain-raiser for a day's dedicated fundraising for the oncology centres in Bristol and Musgrove, was supported by a terrific turnout by the family and friends of Butleigh president Philip Gristock.

Butleigh number eight Duncan Craig, having prepared for this prodigious match with a morning visit to Roger Wilkins' Cider Farm, winced as his fly half once again dropped the ball, giving Tor a scrummage in front of Butleigh's posts.

Trudging through the sodden, treacley, ankle-deep quagmire of a pitch, he remonstrated with the player.

"What is the matter with you?" he shouted, "this pitch is no worse than yours at the Rec in Bath. Is this as good as it gets?"

From the touchline it was difficult to gauge ex-England full back and Bath Rugby Club coach Jon Callard's reaction. Now covered in saturated cloying stained mud, his face was a frozen mask of clay indistinguishable from 29 others on the field of play.

Craig, Scottish to the last pleat of his ancestral kilt along with three million other aggrieved countrymen, had possibly never quite forgiven this same player for the disputed injury time penalty converted from beyond the halfway line in a mid-1990s Murrayfield international that allowed England to snatch an unlikely victory.

Tor, with the advantage of a south westerly gale, scored two early converted tries before their enigmatic prop Paul Lockyer received a controversial stamping in the loose from his second row lock forward Malcolm Dykes. Dykes, on

Butleigh on the attack

top form, later proceeded to rake his fellow powerhouse second row John Marshfield.

Fine handling by Trigger MacNals, Chris Jones and Jon Hunt allowed an opportunity for the Amateurs' flying wing Spencer Hicks to score a crucial try against the elements.

In the second half during a terrific battle of wills, Butleigh scrum half Geoff Landucci and wing forward Warren Dean scored tenacious tries to set up a thrilling finish.

Much later Tim Gelfs, occasional full back who once during a midnight torrential thunderstorm with lightning dancing around his footsteps climbed a stack of neatly folded deckchairs and lay down after a particularly testing day on rugby tour, looked quizzical at

the end of a splendid involvement with the evening's auction of promises.

A string of cultured pearls was captured before Gelfs became involved with the bidding of a meal for four people prepared in your home by the Tor Ladies Rugby Team. In a moment of inspiration and with the bidding anchored on £70 the girls offered to carry out the culinary experience topless.

Gelfs secured the offer with a further £30 but as half of the girls can't cook and the rest are vegetarian, the latter being of particular concern, the offer remains one of fascinated anticipation.

The quite stunning auction brilliantly officiated by Fatty Edwards raised £2,352.65 of

December 14th 2000

The report from the *Central Somerset Gazette* mentions the names of some of the many people who have contributed to fund raising and it shows the huge esteem in which Philip Gristock, former President of Butleigh RFC, was held.

Rugby revels in the mud

LINE-OUT action from a charity rugby match between a Butleigh President's XV and Tor at Glastonbury on Sunday. Proceeds go to the oncology centre at Bristol Royal Infirmary.

Picture by Ian Sumner

which the Butleigh shirt worn by Jon Callard fetched £943. The overall total raised for the oncology centres was in excess of £3,000.

The day was terrific fun with an opportunity for many friends to meet and celebrate this important event. There are many people to acknowledge for the way in which the initial idea was conceived and completed.

To Tor Rugby for staging the day and particularly Tim Kelly, club chairman.

To Fatty Edwards for his amazing auction of promises.

To Claire Gelfs, Lucy Chaddock, Lindsey Craig and Jenny Jones for their terrific help in selling raffle tickets and collecting monies from the auction.

To all the incredibly generous sponsors and those who made such generous donations for the auction and raffle.

To all the players who created an exciting game worthy of the occasion, particularly Jon Callard, fitness coach Mark Spivey and Bath Rugby Club for their generous contributions and support.

To Stephen Gillam and his outstanding Blues Band Fole Fretz who played for the good of the cause to Byron Otton who worked so unstintingly providing excellent meals.

To hero of the day Butleigh president Philip Gristock who chose such excellent good causes for the fundraising and partying till the last song and importantly to Colin Gravatt whose idea of the day it was and whose enthusiasm made the day such a success.

Finally to this newspaper for its influential support.

This Sunday's meeting is at the Rose and Portcullis from noon.

Ashley Maunder

10. Twickenham

Initial visits in a white van meant that passengers travelled three abreast in the front seat. They arrived in the car park at The Winning Post; a pub situated a mile from the ground, to meet up with representatives from both sides, supporters draped in home country shorts, scarves and flags.

Following a few rounds, lunch would be taken in the back of a van with the table up and chairs provided, table cloth laid and a feast of food enjoyed before the walk down to the ground. As the Butleigh club grew in numbers, a minibus would be hired. Fatty Edwards became more adept at finding tickets. A network of clubs and friends built up ticket contacts to go with those of Butleigh, Aller, Tor, Wincanton, Wells and other local clubs. The idea was that you chose which matches you wished to travel to and you could exchange your 'away' tickets to Ireland, Scotland, Wales and France that you didn't want to use. Groups would therefore be arranged for epic weekends away to overseas internationals to take up the pool of tickets. Never in the history of this system has a ticket been sold for more than its face value and they are always sold to a genuine club supporter within the clubs involved. The numbers and popularity grew. Mini buses were sold out, there was magnificent company all day and wondrous singing all the way home.

Heading back from Twickenham at the end of the day it was usual to stop at the Bell at Winterbourne Stoke on Salisbury Plain for further refreshments. Berkeley would produce his guitar and further singing would erupt. Often another rugby team would be there. If England had won it was a noisy, celebratory visit. On this occasion, Minehead Barbarians were already in the Bell and friendly, well recognised faces led thunderous

singing. The Butleigh driver gave a signal to drink up and within another round, twenty minutes or so later, revellers began to leave and sit on the bus. They awaited the stragglers and these included Fatty Edwards and the Butleigh club captain who were involved in a meaningful discussion with the Minehead chairman. Fifteen minutes later as Fatty and the captain left the Bell they found to their dismay the bus had departed without them. 'Leave them behind,' chief mutineer, Mark Wilkinson, had advised. 'They've got a lift back with Minehead.' This, of course, is what happened.

It was a squash getting the two, nearly twenty stone, forwards in the mini bus but most accommodating of the Minehead club to take the extra passengers as far as the outskirts of Ilchester, only ten miles away from Glastonbury and their night's sleep.

Trudging off towards the small town centre at midnight, the duo had an incredible piece of luck in that an empty taxi picked them up and took them back to the captain's home costing them a mere £10. There, over further drinks Fatty started to write his hit list. In a wavering scribble he listed, eventually, the name of everyone who had abandoned them.

Six weeks later the bus travelled once more to Twickenham – packed to the gunnels, another sell out – with a few new faces on board including the legend and future club president Phil Gristock. Phil, sadly, was one of the few that hadn't been involved in the previous trip's abandonment. 'Well,' said Fatty when this point was put to him, 'there's bound to be some friendly fire but we've got to settle this. It won't be easy. They strictly told the driver, Nick Crawley to lock the van and not hand over the keys to anyone.'

The Twickenham trip is a long day and calling in once more, quite late, to the Bell on the way home, suspicion was allayed by drinks and great company and defences were down.

'Any chance of the keys, old chap,' said Fatty Edwards to the driver of the locked vehicle, 'I've left my wallet on the bus.' Fatty, six foot five towered over the elfin driver who, in a moment, forgot his responsibilities.

'Of course.'

'I'll bring them straight back,' said Fatty and, under his breath, 'tomorrow.'

Fatty sidled across the packed room to the captain, 'Right I've got them, come on, we're off.'

'I can't Fatty. We can't leave seventeen people at this time of night.'

'We can,' he said and moved to the exit door where he raised the keys in his right hand and jangled them temptingly before disappearing through the door. The captain wavered no more and, collecting his coat, surreptitiously edged his way, pint in hand for camouflage and slipped out through the same doorway. The bus was parked across a crunching stone car park. It seemed a noisy eternity to reach it, unlock the doors, climb in and start up the diesel engine. They edged the vehicle, tyres crunching, towards the exit, onto the road (still no alarm), a right turn and lights on and away. Apart from the two hijackers, an empty Twickenham bus roared off into the night.

Thrilled, delighted and vindicated Edwards and the captain some two gallons of beer to the good raced into the night.

'We've done it,' roared Edwards with delight. 'We've got our own back on the b******ds. We'll just give them a bit of a fright – we're stopping at the first pub on the left hand side on the way home.' This philosophy was generous hearted – however the next pub turned out to be forty miles further on at the Sparkford Inn, where pints were ordered and they made a phone call to the Bell to find out the fate of the rest of the Twickenham party.

'All hell let loose,' said a barmaid. 'Everyone was blaming you two but it's finally been resolved – they've hired the pub's darts team bus – the landlord's driven them home – but its costing good money. £5 a head.'

'Perfect,' said Fatty. 'That's exactly what our taxi cost when we were abandoned.'

Arriving back at the Rose and Portcullis, Fatty and the captain had the enjoyment of another hour's refreshment before the rest of the Twickenham crowd arrived. Pouring out of the bus it was evident there was a high level of anger, disagreement and aggrieved body language.

'We may be in for a spot of bother,' said the club captain.

'No – look,' said Fatty, 'they're arguing with each other.' Peering through the Rose and Portcullis window at Phil Gristock jumping up and down with rage, almost melting the tarmac, you could hear the problem.

'I've never seen anyone treated so abysmally,' he roared. 'How could you, you ungrateful bunch of …… How could you behave like that when the landlord has kindly driven us all this way back – who started the drinks fight? Who was rude to the landlord? Who?'

'Fantastic,' said Fatty. 'They've all fallen out with each other – they've forgotten all about us.

Fatty Edwards at Play.

That'll teach them,' he threw back his head and laughed until tears appeared.

To travel in the company of Fatty Edwards is a complete rugby experience. There is another good story involving him. Roger Trent, a representative of an animal feed company and a rugby player, once invited a 'handful' of farmers to his company marquee at Twickenham. Fatty suggested that a prodigious number of acquaintances accompany him to this event, all ready to say that they purchased large quantities of cow cake from the firm. Roger had a word with Fatty about these large numbers of people and they moved off to the nearby George Inn.

There they met up with a familiar crowd from the North of England and, after copious gallons of ale, singing and battering of heads with a metal tray; matters became more physical with an arm wrestling contest. This moved on to belly butting as Edwards challenged the largest man in the room. With strips stripped off, the two massive beer bellies collided. A cascade of sweat burst off the two bodies. Fascinated onlookers ducked away, covering their pints of beer in alarm.

The compensation claim by the animal feed firm for the excessive amount of food and drink consumed by Edward's party of 36 was easily responded to by replying that it couldn't be Roger Trent's Blandford Branch fault as he only had four Somerset farmers on his books.

At Twickenham the place to meet is at the Paull's hospitality tent. Here, over a drink and buffet luncheon, tickets for the game are allocated. It is also a hospitable place to meet after the match. In recent years, following the final whistle, the place to go is the Rack and Ruin bar situated within Twickenham's North stand. It is a brilliant place to continue the day. It is where home and away supporters meet. In front of a huge bar, which stays open for two hours after the game, decade defining songs are sung over a karaoke machine. Hundreds of people pile in to sing American Pie, Green Green Grass of Home, Suspicious Minds and Day Dream Believer. In a football stadium, or at Cardiff in the magnificent Millennium stadium on football days, the bars are closed in the stand and pubs are closed within the vicinity. On rugby days there are signs around all the open bars advising that there is a restriction of four pints of beer per person to be taken to their seat at any one time. Stiff cardboard trays are issued to help with the privilege.

Thus Twickenham can be summed up. Supporters mix together, flags and scarves are given to children, hands and arms thrown over shoulders. People sing together and everyone understands that life is bigger than rugby, everyone is generous of heart and spirit and having the time of their lives.

11. Tour of South Africa 2006

The Butleigh Amateurs RFC squad.

Joseph Steadfast-Smythe's moment of inspiration came at breakfast - a late breakfast because sleep the previous evening had been a late affair. However, he had the idea of negotiating with the lively, energetic samba band playing on Cape Town's Waterfront.

Eight hours later, the Butleigh Veterans XV had finally overcome a sprightly City RFC veteran team 35-20.At the same time, the Butleigh 1st XV, captained by Andy Quinlan, was engaged with the Temperance RFC XV. Shortly into the match, Steadfast's musical entourage arrived setting up alongside the Cape Coloured's rugby pitch. The well fortified ground with barbed wire, seven foot high corrugated fencing, a mini Pilton festival barricade, protected a spread eagled 3 pitch ground and floodlit arena. The stand held some eighty home team supporters who sang and chanted for their side. Within ten minutes, two Butleigh tries were scored by centres Trigger MacNab and John Cox with the samba band engaging full percussion rhythm.

Then two things happened. Firstly, it started raining. Secondly, the home side supporters became vocally muted before sidling across the stand, apparently mesmerically transfixed by Steadfast's orchestra. Andrew Joyce added a third try. Will Askam contributed two. Tim Alchin was involved in separate misunderstandings. After match presentations of rugby shirts to the opposition captains led, following a lively evening of Africa Drum and Beat entertainment in the clubhouse, to a minor riot as fights broke out over owner's rights to the multi-coloured shirts given as presents.

The following evening's farewell dinner for 36 tourists in Longstreet Cape Town, imaginatively organised by Tim Gelfs and Tim Alchin, exceeded all expectations. 'What happened to the budget?' shouted aggrieved tour organiser, Andy Nixon. 'We haven't got £1,200!' The seven course meal, in the wall and ceiling carpeted Kurdish restaurant, including hot chilli kidneys and lambs testicles accompanied by a sizeable barrel of red wine in the candlelit, incense filled room, was not wholly responsible for the doubling of the agreed allowance.

The not unattractive belly dancer, Miss Eloa Shaka, was. She demonstrated gyrations, vibrations and suppleness beyond nature's hopes and then retired to thunderous applause. Miss Shaka was considered an excellent investment and she danced, after a splendid solo floor show, with everyone. The main distraction of the evening, however, was provided by the arrival of the Sheshka Kurdish smoking pots which resembled large brass Edwardian gas lamps. These communal smoking urns, accompanied by a metre of supple snake like hose, came complete with a wooden bag pipe like mouth piece. After twenty minutes of activity within the dining room with the touring team sitting, just beyond the no smoking signs, cross-legged on cushions on the floor, Colonel Ian Saunders appeared to be producing excessive billows of smoke from his pot so that each person eventually lost sight of the others in a cloud of liquorish tasting fog.

Leaving at a disciplined 8am the following morning the tourists caught a connecting flight to sub tropical Durban. Butleigh's next match is with Winterton RFC on Wednesday in the heart of the Drakensberg Mountains – Zulu country.

Drakensberg RFC 34
Butleigh RFC 19 10th May 2006

Arriving in Durban on the second leg of their tour, the 36 strong party travelled two hundred miles inland towards Winterton, a small farming town situated at the foot of the Drakensberg mountains. Over the six hour journey the terrain became less fertile. Willowy reed grasses replaced plantations of sugar cane and maize. Fewer animals were seen. The vista, isolation, sparse population, remoteness, distance, mountains all epitomise Zulu country. Indigenous houses, circular brown thatched turrets, lay as scattered handfuls of brown thrown buttons – each with a washing line, brightly filled, half tethered in scratchy, cropped gardens. Smoke plumes drifted from mushroom shaped roofs. For the rural inhabitants there is no chance whatsoever of economic progress. Caught in an existence of under-populated poverty is the evolving culture of this vast, awesome region of South Africa.

Fifty miles short of our lodgings at Cathedral Peak Hotel we stop at Winterton, a dry, red earthed town where the next day's rugby match is to be played. Drakensberg rugby club looks homely, the pitch lined with maple trees gives a feeling of how Butleigh's pitch may look in years to come. Wind rustles through the leaves. Very poignant; stirs thoughts of friends at home.

The club house is a modern, long, single storied building with an elegant maroon tiled floor. A heavy, deeply shining mahogany bar runs the length of

one side of the room flanked by banks of beer chiller cabinets. Drakensberg players are Afrikaans farmers, tough as teak, coached by former Springbok fly half, Henry Honniball's brother. The next day's match is the talk of the area. Everyone tells us its going to be a hard game. They play in the equivalent of South West One and have won their league for the last two years. Butleigh however have a number of former county players in their squad and many other younger players who play Western Counties or Somerset premiership rugby. Back onto the coach and the road snakes upwards arriving an hour later at Cathedral Peak Hotel set 5000 feet above sea level in the heart of the most stunningly beautiful scenery imaginable.

The following day's match back at Winterton is tough, fast and uncompromising. Butleigh struggle to contain the Drakensberg three-quarter line. Two tries in twelve minutes from either wing leave the visitors ten points adrift. However, Butleigh scrum half Tom Collins sends Trigger Macnab through a defensive gap passing to wing Will Askham who brings the ball back inside to supporting lock forward Tim Alchin who passes to tight head prop Paul Lockyer who, evading two tackles, scores under the posts. Trigger converts. 10 – 7. Two further tries and a penalty move the home side to a half time 27 – 7 lead. A courageous second half performance, however, led by captain Andy Quinlan, allows Butleigh, through their forwards, to firstly maul Quinlan over for a try followed by a penalty try awarded when Butleigh front row Mike Rodgers, Simon Hall and Paul Lockyer and the rest of the pack scrummage their Drakensberg opposition back through their own posts where they illegally collapse the scrum.

In the after match revelries, Fatty Edwards failed in an attempt to charm our truly excellent tour guide for three days Miss Fiona Brookfield-Legget with Allouetta necessitating a change of femme fatale shortly after the normally winning verse of how he loves her swinging bits. However Fatty's near masterstroke was in taking on the home side 6'8", fifty two year old, twenty four stone president, the splendidly named Gunter Muller, an Afrikaans German who not only dwarfed Edwards in stature but, more worryingly, could allegedly down a pint in two seconds. Edwards, on peak form in a shrewd manoeuvre challenged Gunter to a pint in one, standing upside down in a handstand, back against the wall. Edwards, who is surprisingly athletic with one good man pinning his legs against the wall, achieved his time, eight seconds. With Gunter, the problem lay in getting this mammoth man upside down with legs in the air; a gymnastic feat which he had never before attempted. Surrounded by a fascinated, cheering crowd Gunter attempted the handstand, first with the aid of one assistant. Following three crashing efforts, spread eagling the crowd each time, three men pinned him to the clubhouse wall and the drink was attempted. Six seconds – a thunderous cheer – Edwards however was having none of it.

'You dribbled,' he said, wiping a fleck of froth off the huge man's top lip. 'You'll have to go again.'

Roared on by the vibrant crowd Gunter was hauled once more onto the wall. Still Edwards was not satisfied.

'It's no good. A drip's just rolled off your nose.' Three times Gunter Muller handstanded a pint in one until finally, to vast acclaim, he was declared 'Down-in-one, upside-down Champion of Winterton'.

Durban Falcons RFC 17
Butleigh Amateur RFC 34

Returning to Durban for the third leg of Butleigh's tour, a trip to Kings Park Stadium was arranged to see a Super Fourteen match between the Natal Sharks and Perth's Western Force. Following Butleigh's midweek game, the President of Drakensberg rugby Club, Günter Muller, having won his 'three pints in one' drinking competition offered tickets to the four largest men in the Butleigh squad to his personal hospitality box for the match. Gunter likes big men. Although it was more intimate than usual and the bar within the box had to be restocked three times during the match, the twenty one Butleigh players that gained access reported well of the experience.

After the game the Butleigh squad adjourned to the 'Eighties Night Club' situated within Kings Park stadium, before moving to the city's casino where it became evident that Colonel Ian Saunders excellent touring form was undiminished. Not only had he survived, suffering only a bruised shoulder, being run over late one night but had thrived in heavy seas viewing shark from a submerged cage five miles off Cape Town. He had also partly resolved a communications misunderstanding with his long suffering, incredibly patient wife, six thousand miles away in England, over a text intercepted by Trigger MacNab.

The Colonel, whilst taking refreshments with friends elsewhere, had somewhat neglectfully left his phone on a table that included Macnab as a guest. The Colonel's wife, in a moment of fondness, had, in the text, suggested that her husband's performance the night before leaving for South Africa merited the accolade of 'sex pot'. Trigger, in the Colonel's absence, thoughtfully replied that such would be the passion on his (the Colonel's) return that he would render her senseless which, he added somewhat controversially, would be easily achieved since she didn't have any. Having sent the text, Trigger then ordered a substantial round of drinks on the Colonel's bar tab instructing the waiter to navigate the bar calling in a firm voice for the 'Sex pot' to settle his account.

With these distractions only a few days behind him, Saunders very sensibly waited in the casino until daybreak allowing the early morning light to assist in the walk back to the hotel. Accompanying him were Brooking Clark and Will Askham. Nearing the hotel the Colonel, by now striding purposefully along the beach promenade, decided on an early morning swim in the nearby Indian Ocean and, without pause for the sensibilities of man or beast, stripped to nothing and marched towards the surf and Madagascar.

Returning from the sea there was however disappointment concerning the whereabouts of his clothes which, along with his companions, were missing. Stumbling along the beach in fruitless search Saunders came across a number of senior citizens taking the early morning air and a prayer group holding a service on the sands. Resourceful tactics eventually furnished him with a fallen palm leaf but the sanctuary of his residence at the Blue Waters Hotel, far away across a busy dual carriageway, still lay a quarter of a mile in the distance.

Tour Captain Andy Quinlan.

Later that evening, Butleigh's final match kicked off at the impressive Durban Falcons rugby ground. Two pitches, floodlights, grandstand, swish clubhouse overlooking a glittering light-spangled city with family BBQs and background music along the touchlines greeted our arrival. The pace of the game seemed as furious as the Winterton match but with James Phillips moving from full-back to scrum half and supplying a three quarter line of Moose, Andrew Joyce, Tom Collins, John Cox and Will Askham, with Trigger playing full back, a game full of flair from both sides evolved. Captain Andy Quinlan scored, as he had in every match, a vital try. There were also touchdowns for Collins, Rodgers, Askham, Lockyer and Brooking Clarke as Butleigh came from 17-14 down midway through the second half, to take the game.

Moments of individual initiative throughout the week include Joseph Steadfast Smythe's hiring of the band that arrived at Butleigh's first match and setting up on the touchline played high tempo Caribbean music to enliven the team's performance. Further initiatives followed. A barren four hour fishing trip was overseen by a warden. When he retired from the scene, Chris White and Steadfast switched direction, casting successfully over a seven foot high fence into the nearby out of bounds trout farm. The resulting catch was prepared by the hotel for dinner that evening. Quite outstanding, however, was the doubling of the £600 budget for the Cape Town dinner organised by Tim Alchin and Tim Gelfs at the Kurdish restaurant and the hiring of vibrant belly dancer, Miss Eloa Shaka.

Leaving for Heathrow on the back of eleven days' touring that included abseiling, quad biking, battlefield visits, fishing, golf, surfing, paintballing, cage diving, fantastic rugby, horse riding within awesome scenery tempered with the realities of visiting the Soul of Africa orphanage and Nelson Mandela's prison cell on Robben Island, it is appropriate to mention Butleigh's quite magnificent tour organiser, Andy Nixon, by whom this whole incredible adventure was staged.

Butleigh RFC Charity Donation to the Soul of Africa
A visit to the Khulani Children's Shelter, run by Mike and Sarah Gedge and situated within Durban's Park Hill suburb allowed Butleigh Rugby Club to present a cheque for five hundred pounds to the Soul of Africa Children's Charity.

The shelter was founded by Prudence Mwandla. She cared for young children left abandoned at Durban railway station by parents either too ill with Aids or who drifted off seeking work. Following a visit by Lance Clark, a link had been forged initially with Clark's shoe foundation in England. Lance, while on a visit to assist and advise the South African footwear association, was introduced to the Khulani Shelter which at the time housed 85 children struggling in one bungalow with one toilet and one washroom. With generous financial support from the Clarks Family Trust, a crèche was created to care for the youngest children whilst Khulani was upgraded to care for those aged 7-16. It gives comfort, educational skills, computer literacy skills and employment opportunities when children leave the centre.

Aids affects a large proportion of the African population and many children are born carrying the condition. Many sadly die by the age of five. All the children supported by Khulani are Aids free but come from traumatic family situations. In this caring environment they sparkle with confidence. Butleigh's donation will be used to help develop two more shelters within Durban and to help the work to continue in the years ahead. The monies for the donation were raised at Butleigh's Magnificent 7's Rugby Tournament last August Bank Holiday under the inspirational flair of Butleigh Chairman, Colin Gravatt. The club will follow the development of the shelters with great interest.

Club members at the Khulani Shelter.

12. Long, Long Time Ago...

In the Holy Trinity Church, Walton, people in dark jackets, white shirts with black ties or maroon and multi coloured rugby shirts, as bright as stained glass windows, moved quietly to their seats. The church was full; groups standing at the back felt comforted in their closeness as Butleigh president Philip John Gristock's family and friends drew near to give the great man a service of farewell in one of the saddest but most complete funerals imaginable. Hundreds more gathered outside the church as hymns, The Lord is my Shepherd and Abide with Me were sung. Tears, gentle as dew, fell personally, silently.

The man was simply magnificent, six foot six tall. He had a close, loving family. He was a prison officer who captained the prison service national team and he played for many teams including Butleigh Amateurs and Tor. Above all, Philip could sing – beautifully. Known affectionately as the human juke box, there was not an Irish ballad or a rock and roll classic that he could not perform. His favourite music was Buddy Holly and the Berkeley, Gillam, Pursey Trio. Can you imagine how much this man brought to the Butleigh club when he first played in 1984?

A passionate England supporter, one of his best days ever was travelling to Twickenham to see England beat France in the Grand Slam decider in 1991. The Winning Post public house, a mile from the ground, rang out to the gods that night as he reeled off song after song to a thronging and deliriously happy crowd.

A man of humour, dignity, strength, wisdom and great loyalty; the day he was created they truly broke the mould and it seems unlikely that there will ever be another like him. For many people, he was their mentor in life.

During the service, the most poignant of addresses was given by the prison chaplain, Mike Peters, bringing further images of Philip into our minds. Following a commendation and a blessing, the poem 'Remember' was read by the Reverend Creed. At the end of the service, uniformed prison officers slowly moved to lift the coffin, shouldering their great friend to take him onwards with enormous dignity.

Philip's family, Sandra, Mark and Jo followed, supported by their closest family and friends and Howie Davis, wearing Philip's Butleigh Rugby Club president's waistcoat, accompanied them. Quietly playing in the background and filtering gently through the church was Phillip's favourite song, 'American Pie.'

Five hours later, in the Rose and Portcullis, the song was no longer being whispered. It was being sung to the rafters as Tony Berkeley led the packed Butleigh pub which was bursting at the seams in a celebration of Philip's life.

Lung bursting renditions of 'Running Bear', 'Wild Rover' and the Six Nations filled ears, minds and senses with an intensity that everyone felt for Philip and his family.

The pace of singing and strumming was such that guitar strings started popping with such alarming frequency that following one more stunning rendition, Berkeley, fingers numb with note changes, was left staring forlornly at a bouquet of splayed guitar strings.

The team that raised funds for the Bristol Oncology Unit.

A week later, a match with Milborne Port refereed by Fatty Edwards featured the Butleigh Union Jack flying at half mast whilst both teams held a minute's silence. On a warm Autumn afternoon, with families together, children running free and easy conversation over wine and rugby, it was just the place that Phil would have wanted to be, which, indeed, he is. One of his final wishes was that his ashes should be scattered on the Kingweston pitch.

An oak tree has been planted in his memory alongside a commemorative wooden bench with a view across the ground.

Philip's tree is not alone. Over the last three decades, other wonderful players and friends have passed on and each one has a tree planted in their memory. Each one had a life as special and unique as Philip's and each one is remembered over a raised glass with the greatest love and affection. Maybe all of them are somewhere together.

Sandra Gristock and Colin Gravatt planting a tree in memory of Philip.

. . . and into the future

As a team, Butleigh has travelled and enjoyed fixtures and due weight has been given to the varied influences of players and characters joining the club. Everyone has a chance to express their wishes and usually to follow them through. Rugby tours began in Brighton and now they have moved through Spain to South Africa. All this happened because people expressed a wish to travel and then they were prepared to do the graft and research to enable those epic touring adventures to materialize.

David Chadburn organised the first tour, Robin and Rupert Reid introduced Spain and President Tony Berkeley developed this link with a passion over twenty years. Tony has always been a family and friends orientated organiser and subsequent visits to Spain meant that strong ties with many Spanish families have been forged, some as strong as our friendships with each other over here. Andy Nixon has taken the club twice to South Africa; the most stunning, beguiling and challenging rugby country imaginable. With detailed research, and by assembling a particularly useful playing squad, Butleigh have won 5 out of 7 games. Unbelievable!

Stephen Gillam, who founded the Magnificent Sevens August bank holiday tournament, has seen it prosper and progress into one of the counties biggest seven - a - side charity competitions under the energy and organisational skills of Chairman Colin Gravatt.

After a number of early years of gentle, humour-filled anarchy with the Somerset RFU authorities, the arrival of club secretary Chris Harding instilled, with proper insurance and regular attendance at RFU meetings, a respectful working relationship with two way communication with the Somerset RFU administration. Thanks to Harding's vocal support in front of seven hundred delegates at the NEC Birmingham, Butleigh has been recognised and invited on a regular basis to compete in the City Sevens Charity Rugby Tournament held at Deer Park in Richmond. Butleigh is the only club outside the city financial institutions rugby scene to be invited.

The Cup rugby matches are a highlight of each season. Neither Butleigh, nor the Cup opposition, virtually until the moment of kick off, are quite sure of the make up of the Butleigh team. The end of season Black Tie Summer Ball celebrates the end of one season and the opening of another on August Bank Holiday Friday. This wonderful event is now staged in a vast marquee on our own home pitch.

The mighty Rose and Portcullis public house has patiently, through four sets of landlords in thirty years, served us so well. It provides a hospitable, social scene where conversations, dreams and celebrations have been fulfilled.

And to the future – games on a Sunday, interspersed with more midweek floodlit matches, seems to be the way. Wednesday evenings seem particularly popular. Last season Butleigh played Taunton, Bridgwater, Ivel Barbarians, Swanage and Wareham, North Dorset and Milborne Port, all away under lights; terrific fun with the best of facilities on offer and played by players without hangovers against guaranteed full XV opposition.

A further overseas tour will be announced shortly and the usual excitements of the Christmas Feast and Easter Monday rugby extravaganza at the legendary Barton Inn will continue to flourish.

Most promising of all though might be the future for Butleigh Amateur Rugby Club through the stunningly successful TAG rugby on Tuesday nights on the playing field at Butleigh. Conceived out of a conversation between Butleigh school representative Ruth Higgins and Butleigh International Pip Kennedy, eighty children and teenagers turn out every Tuesday to play in this thrilling youth activity. With support from Colin Gravatt, Ian Innes and Andy Foot everyone between the ages of six and sixty can play. Since the early days, three teenagers - Ashley Hill, Matt Holsworth and Paul Harwood have come through to play for the club.

The future? To remain the same – no change – to retain the status quo – to enjoy every game as it comes, to allow time in the bar for the day to mature, to accept life as it is and to enjoy everyone's company within the very best days of our sporting lives.

Tag Rugby at Butleigh playing field

List of subscribers to the first edition

1. Adam Maunder
2. Janet & Dennis Powell
3. June Richards
4. Puddy's Bakery
5. Colin Reason-Winston
6. Roger Ward
7. Big Jay
8. Joe Newton
9. Lucy Chaddock
10. Eurwyn Roberts
11. Jade Olivia Passmore
12. Hollie May Passmore
13. Sandra Gristock
14. Damon & Anita
15. Geoff Berry
16. Tom Smith
17. Christopher Greenwood MBE
18. A. Quinlan
19. Antonia Maunder
20. Dudley Tremaine
21. Percy Gane
22. Kim Gane
23. Mark Twentyman
24. Buff Powell
25. Chris Jones
26. Patrick Baker
27. Christian Hughes
28. Ian Saunders
29. David Kelly
30. Peter Thorner
31. Pat & Dennis Thorner
32. David Biles
33. Alan Aylett
34. Tim
35. Derek
36. Alison
37. Brian Cheeseman
38. Russell Croker
39. Richard Long
40. George Weaver
41. Ben Fenner
42. Stanley Hoole
43. Ken Newport
44. Chas Newport
45. Tim & Claire Gelfs
46. The Revd. Stuart M. Munns
47. Tony Phelps
48. Lord Hawker
49. Joshua Sharpe
50. Martin & Elaine Shute
51. Oliver & Jacob Stafford
52. Owen & Christine Powell
53. Jon & Carol Ashley
54. Jenny & Fred Govier
55. Julia Maunder
56. Murray Eaglesome
57. Colin Gravatt
58. Johnnie
59. Mary Cooper
60. Karen & John Dixon

61. Mark Lewis

62. Gladys Stevenson

63. Gordon & Evelyn

64. The Rose & Portcullis

65. Steve Gillam

66. Andrew Foot

67. Kevin Stock

68. Bridget, Emma &
    Ryan Passmore

69. Mark Nicholson-Lailey

70. Simon Davies

71. Bernard Stacey

72. Colin Dickens

73. Chris Harding

74. Jules & Adrian

75. Simon & Jools

76. Helen & Mike

77. Richard Heath

78. R. L. Breeds

79. Suzanna Maunder

80. Jon Fear

81. Dick Fear

82. Graham Burr

83. Heidi Pope
    Rose & Portcullis Bar Maid

84. Marilyn Fletcher

85. Dennis Speed

86. Alan Charles

87. Sarah Higgins

88. Rick Cook

89. Anne Campbell

90. E. G. Coombes

91. Caroline Coombes

92. Paul Tuckett

93. Andy Frecknall

94. Sue Fletcher

95. Tracey & Eirian

96. J. Goodman

97. Andrew Hill

98. Cliff Taylor

99. Peter Farrant

100. Andy Nixon

101. Nick Schanche

102. Trevor Greenhill

103. Margaret Grundy

104. Paul Lockyer

105. Darran Porter

106. David & Jane Sedgman

107. Tim Kelly Jnr.

108. Jon Fear

109. Harry Buckle Jnr.

110. Harry Buckle

111. Sarah Broom

112. Jo Pitman

113. Jean Parry

114. James Phillips

115. Andy Wall

116. Keith & Marcia Richards

117. Brian Harbinson

118. Richard & Fay Robinson

119. Leslie & Ayesha Foot

120. The Somerton Printery Ltd

Stop Press

News

Rugby referee's World Cup selection joy

Sports editor Clare Daniels

It was not just Italians who were celebrating success this week as Mid Somerset Newspapers' sports editor Clare Daniels received some World Cup good news of her own.

Clare, a rugby union referee in her spare time, has been selected to referee in this year's Women's Rugby World Cup in Canada, with the tournament kicking off at the end of August.

The event will see 12 teams from across the globe battle it out for the title of World Champions, presently held by the New Zealand Black Ferns, with England ranked second favourites.

The three-week competition will be staged in Edmonton and Clare is one of eight women referees selected to officiate at the event by the International Rugby Board (IRB).

Clare, a member of the Somerset Referees' Society, said: "I'm over the moon, to be honest, and can't wait to get out there.

"I've had the World Cup in my sights for more than two years, and have worked hard with that in mind.

"Anybody involved in sport will know that you dream of representing your country, so I'm thrilled to be doing just that on a World Cup stage.

"It's great that the IRB has selected women officials to work alongside the men they appointed, and proves that women's rugby is a growing sport.

"I've had a lot of support from the guys in the Society and RFU and can't thank them all enough. I've got to fly the flag for Somerset and the RFU now and make sure I do the job to the best of my ability."

IRB referees' manager and ex-international official Paddy O'Brien said: "This selection represents the greatest number of women officials ever appointed for an IRB Tournament.

"It is also encouraging to note that there is also a broad representation of Unions, with officials from nine countries appointed.

"The Women's Rugby World Cup represents a great opportunity for the best women players to showcase their talents in a major tournament on the international stage, and the same can be said for the match officials.

"The selection committee was extremely impressed by the standard of nominations received and those appointed have an opportunity to continue their development in an international tournament environment."

Clare was recently appointed to the South West Group of referees, and is the first female in the country to make the cut at level five league rugby. She will be joined in Canada by touch judge Debbie Innes from Gloucester.

Running Fox

Running Fox assists authors to self-publish their work. Advice and practical help can be given at different stages of the process and costs vary according to the requirements of each individual. Books appearing under this imprint include a family history based on a collection of letters, reminiscences about the local area and a forthcoming volume of short stories.

Running Fox has appreciated working closely on this particular venture with The Somerton Printery and with illustrator Jeff Farrow as well as with the author, Ashley Maunder. E-mail Janet Powell for further information on janet@runningfox.co.uk or leave your contact details with The Somerton Printery.